MAN OF ARMOUR

Rommel as Military Commander
Montgomery as Military Commander
Churchill as War Lord
Freedom's Battle: The War on Land, 1939–1945 (Ed.)

MAN
OF ARMOUR

A study of
LIEUT-GENERAL VYVYAN POPE
and the development of
armoured warfare

by
RONALD LEWIN

LEO COOPER · LONDON

First published in Great Britain 1976 by
LEO COOPER LTD
196 Shaftesbury Avenue, London WC2H 8JL

Copyright © 1976 by Ronald Lewin

ISBN 0 85052 050 9

Printed in Great Britain by
Western Printing Services Ltd
Bristol

CONTENTS

ACKNOWLEDGEMENTS

My text reveals the central importance of Pope's private papers for his biographer. For prolonged access to them, for permission to quote from his unpublished writings and for much help and encouragement, I am greatly indebted to his widow, Mrs Vyvyan Pope and his son Michael Pope.

Others from whom I have received invaluable advice and information are Major-General H. L. Birks, Major-General the Viscount Bridgeman, Major-General Raymond Briggs, Major-General Nigel Duncan, Major-General Sir Charles Dunphie, Colonel Peter Dunphie, Major-General Lionel Finch, E. B. Gordon, Major-General H. M. Liardet, Major Kenneth Macksey, Captain Reginald Minchin, Lieut-General the Lord Norrie, General Sir Richard O'Connor, Sir Charles Petrie, Bt., Lieut-General Maurice Pope, Major-General Douglas Wimberley, Lieut-General Sir Arthur Smith, the Rev A. G. Willis and the late Colonel S. J. Worsley.

R.L.

ILLUSTRATIONS

CHAPTER ONE

THE START-LINE

At the battle of Naseby in 1645 the left wing of the King's army was commanded by Sir Marmaduke Langdale. Nearly three centuries later, in the winter of 1941, the left wing of another King's army would have been commanded by Sir Marmaduke's kinsman had he not been tragically killed on the very eve of battle. When General Auchinleck formed his Eighth Army for Operation CRUSADER, the offensive which was designed to destroy Rommel's *Afrika Korps* and relieve Tobruk, the man he chose to lead the armoured forces on his desert flank was Lieutenant-General Vyvyan Pope, CBE, DSO, MC, who through his mother Blanche Langdale could trace his lineage back to the cavalier of Naseby. But whereas in that famous battle of the Civil War Sir Marmaduke's horsemen were overwhelmed by Cromwell's superior numbers, in CRUSADER, so it seemed, Pope might well have shattered the panzers of the *Afrika Korps*. His great experience in armour, his ideas about how tanks should be manoeuvred in action, both promised that at last the British might gain ascendancy in the desert. But it was not to be. A plane crash reduced Vyvyan Pope to a reference in the history books.

It is an unfortunate fact that the main way for an officer to become widely known is to win (or sometimes to lose) a battle. Montgomery is a household word, but what of Robertson or Lindsell, without whose organization behind

1

the lines there would never have been a march from Alamein to beyond the Rhine? In proportion to those who have heard of Slim, how many are aware of the Major-General in charge of his supplies, Alf Snelling, of whose 'incredible achievements' Slim wrote with such warmth? Even the man in the street is conscious of George Patton, but nobody will ever make a film about George Marshall. Staff officers are usually faceless men—unless, like Clausewitz, they write a masterpiece.

But the most cruel fate is that of the fighting soldier prevented by circumstance from making a reputation in the field, and no one is more bitterly robbed than he who has successfully dedicated his life to arms, has reached the point where he is about to put his whole career to the test, and at that moment is cheated by death of the chance of glory. This was Pope's—and perhaps his country's—tragedy.

It was not that there was nothing to show for more than a quarter of a century's soldiering, simply that newspaper editors and historians are seldom drawn to promote or discuss generals who have not been picked out by the dramatic light of the battlefield. Yet Pope deserves far more than the footnotes or other incidental references which he has so far received. He was of high class—a man whom a future VCIGS (Sir Archibald Nye) marked down as a future CIGS, and whom another distinguished armoured commander (Major-General Nigel Duncan) thought eminently fit to command the Eighth Army. He was one of that small group of officers who started the First World War as very young men, fought in all the great battles and grew in stature as their capacity and survival thrust them upwards, prematurely, into taxing senior commands. Some stagnated thereafter, but Pope, though lacking a right arm since 1918, joined the embryonic Royal Tank Corps, and from then on his own development as a soldier marched step by step with the development in Great Britain of the 'armoured idea'. It was wholly fitting, therefore, that after two decades of intimate experience of mobile warfare he should have gone out, before Dunkirk, as Armoured Adviser to Lord Gort, and after Dunkirk should have been charged, as Director of Armoured Fighting Vehicles, with the herculean task of handling all the problems involved in building up, almost from scratch, the vital new Armoured Divisions. Pope and armour, in fact, advanced side by side.

His start-line was characteristic: throughout the First War he was an infantry officer. It is often forgotten how few of those who acted as pioneers of armour during the 'twenties and 'thirties, or achieved fame in mobile operations during the Second World War, actually began their careers in tanks—how few, indeed, had served at Cambrai or in the great tank actions of 1918. The spearhead, Major-General Sir Percy Hobart, was a Sapper who did not transfer to the RTC until 1923, the same year as another pioneer, George Lindsay, from the Rifle Brigade. Sir Richard O'Connor, who conducted the most outstanding British armoured operation of the Second World War, the winter offensive of 1940–1941 which swept along the North African shore and destroyed an Italian army, was also a junior infantry officer in 1914 and, like Pope, rose to command a battalion. Horrocks, whose name will always be associated with the 'left hook' round the Mareth Line in 1943 and the gallop to Brussels and Antwerp in 1944, was a subaltern in the Middlesex Regiment when he was captured in October, 1914, to spend the next four years as an escape-prone prisoner of war. Still, the same was so in Germany; Guderian only entered the game in the 'twenties, and Rommel not until he took over his 7th Panzer Division in February, 1940.

The truth is that those who were to fertilize and exploit

3

the armoured idea had common characteristics rather than common origins. (Indeed, if evidence were wanted that no specific background is necessary to become a tank-man it could be found in that successful conversion which produced the Guards Armoured Division, of which, before it succeeded, one could only say *credo quia impossibile*.) They are qualities which, as his story unfolds, will be seen emerging in Vyvyan Pope—imagination, flexibility of mind, realism, meticulous attention to detail, an affinity with machines, a certain *panache* and dislike of the orthodox, courage, and that *tact des choses possibles* which is born of intense experience on the battlefield.

Imagination is a key word. At his preparatory school, Ascham in Eastbourne,* Pope as a small boy had the gift of telling cliffhanger stories *extempore* after Lights Out, night after night. The Rev Arthur Willis, who was his contemporary at school and later became its headmaster, (while Pope's only son Michael was there), recalled in 1972 that, 'I was an athlete and not very imaginative or morally brave. Vyvyan was almost my opposite: sound physically but not an athlete, highly imaginative and morally brave'. That might be any small boy: but unlike so many boys as they mature and conform, Pope contrived to retain a private inner world in which entirely unmilitary values flourished. Neither his public school years at Lancing nor a career in the Regular Army quelled his imagination or stereotyped his mind.

When Hobart was in India in 1907 as a young subaltern in the 1st Bengal Sappers and Miners his first company commander approved of him, but told him that 'he was sorry he had felt bound in conscience to enter an adverse remark on my annual Confidential Report: "This officer is addicted to the reading of poetry."' So, all his life, was

* Pope was born on 30 September, 1891, in London where his father, James Pope, was in the Civil Service.

Pope. Indeed stimulated by Aldous Huxley's *Texts and Pretexts,* he compiled over the years his own *Personal Anthology,* for, like Wavell, he found refreshment and strength in the contemplation of other men's flowers. And Major-General Horace Birks, one of the 'Cambrai originals', noted that when Pope arrived in the Tank Corps there was one thing about him which the men failed to comprehend: he listened to *classical music.*

The result was introversion. Pope was a man of great reserve, *renfermé,* and though his career and his military thinking may be easily read, a biographer finds it less easy to connect his private world with his public performance. Like Wavell, whose favourite contribution to conversation or conference was 'I see' but who always had much going on in his head, Pope was by no means the typical regular officer of his day. Yet, whereas it has been argued that Ian Hamilton's performance at Gallipoli was indecisive because his aesthetic interests had softened him, no one could say that Pope, or Hobart, or indeed the enduring Wavell were diminished as soldiers by their concern for the arts. On the contrary, each, in his idiosyncratic way, benefited from his predilections by not becoming hidebound in his military profession.

In the halcyon summer of 1914 2nd Lieutenant V. V. Pope was the junior officer on the strength of the 1st Battalion The North Staffordshire Regiment. They were stationed at Buttevant in County Cork, as part of the 17th Brigade of the 6th Division. Not surprisingly, their preoccupation was not with the Continent but with the consequences of the Curragh Mutiny. 'I myself had no doubt where my duty lay,' Pope noted. 'I sympathized with Ulster and I distrusted the South, but I could not agree that resort to armed force was legitimate.' There had been no question of surrendering commissions or any form of pressure in this particular Brigade, but there was a prevalent sense of unease, so that when the Battalion was out training one day and a newspaper was suddenly produced its significance was misinterpreted. The main headline read: 'KING'S OWN SCOTTISH BORDERERS FIRE ON CROWD IN DUBLIN: WOMAN KILLED', while beside it was the simple announcement: 'AUSTRIA DECLARES WAR ON SERBIA'. The date was 30 July. 'We were in no doubt as to the relative importance of these two pronouncements; Austria was remote and Serbia remoter; Dublin very near.'

The announcement of a Precautionary Period, followed by mobilization orders, soon dispelled any illusions, as did the arrival of reservists. Young Pope, accustomed to a No. 9 Platoon of perhaps twenty striplings, now suddenly discovered that he was the father and mother of fifty old sweats. He was lucky, as a dedicated professional soldier, to find himself at the start of his career a member of a notably good battalion—one of the sterling elements in that Old Army which was virtually eliminated by the autumn of 1915 and which the Germans used to describe as 'a perfect thing apart'. Pope was fortunate because—as only those who have experienced it can fully understand—the young officer in war is profoundly conditioned by the ethos of his unit. The daily habit of taking for granted high standards of discipline, efficiency and morale has an imperceptible but cumulative effect, and particularly so on a perceptive (and receptive) personality like Pope's. He was lucky, too, in that these very qualities enabled his battalion —with which he was to serve throughout the war—to sustain crippling losses over and over again and yet, by some extraordinary and barely credible process, to renew itself perpetually, a constant Phoenix emerging into new life from the holocausts of the Somme and Passchendaele.

Mobilization certainly revealed some encouraging attitudes. 'It was quite clear that inoculation was voluntary, but the Colonel, with memories of South Africa to support him, was determined that every officer and man in the Battalion should be inoculated. He paraded all ranks, therefore, and very simply but firmly explained the necessity for inoculation, adding that only men who had been inoculated were fit to go to France, in his opinion. If there were any man foolish enough and selfish enough to refuse inoculation, then he would have no alternative but to leave him behind.' The Colonel and every other officer was then inoculated in front of the parade. Only two men from the whole Battalion refused to be jabbed— and those two very soon conformed.

The same principles were applied to officers' kits. All valises were collected in front of the Quartermaster's stores and weighed publicly: an ounce over-weight and the valise was opened, the owner then having to remove his possessions until the correct amount was registered. When the process was completed, all kits were stowed on a wagon and left untouchable under the guard of a sentry. Pope and his fellow subalterns were delighted to watch senior officers, and particularly the Adjutant, being compelled to discard precious but unauthorized articles. 'These measures', he wrote, 'set the tone for the Battalion and we realized that the Colonel intended to keep to the strictest letter of the law, that the law was the same for all, and that no departure from it would be tolerated.' On the whole this was a more constructive approach than that of the Colonel commanding another regular battalion which at this moment was mobilizing in Shorncliffe, the 1st Royal Warwickshire Regiment in which the future Field-Marshal Montgomery was then a Lieutenant. 'The C.O.', Montgomery recalled in his *Memoirs*, 'said that in war it was advisable to have short hair since it was then easier to keep it clean; he had all his hair removed with the clippers by the regimental barber.'

7

Pope's private narrative* of the experiences which began with mobilization in Southern Ireland in 1914 (and took him through the fiery furnace of the next four years, then to North Russia, and then back to an embattled Ireland), is an exceptional document. 'During those seven years of war', he wrote, 'I had lived more intensely than I am ever likely to do again and a sensitive and retentive memory has enabled me to recall not merely what I did but what I thought and felt when doing it.' Others, of course, have succeeded with a similar recall—Sassoon, Blunden, Graves. But they, who lifted routine narration into the region of art, were but 'warriors for the working day'—Hostilities Only soldiers in a Citizen Army. 'It is much more difficult to discover, at the regimental level (the trench level), the record of the Regular Soldier. Generals and Field-Marshals committed millions of words to paper, and very interesting many of them are. But they do not show how the men who were trained for war, brought up to expect war, and soldiered on, with or without war, faced those same situations that Graves, Sassoon and the rest have so graphically described. Did their training make them different men? If so, in what did the difference lie? ... Were they dull fellows? Were they less sensitive to death and suffering than their Citizen comrades? Did they ever give way? Did they have doubts and regrets? What was it that sustained them?' So John Terraine introduced his edition of one of the few records extant of a regular soldier's mind in battle.† It is the merit of Pope's memoir that he answers Terraine's questions even more satisfactorily than does General Jack. The young Staffordshire subaltern was not only a man of action (as the next chapter demonstrates): he had the triple extra qualities of being able to observe, to brood on what he had

* *The Great War as seen by a Regimental Officer; a Fragment of Autobiography.*

† *General Jack's Diary, 1914–1918*, edited by John Terraine, Eyre and Spottiswoode, 1964.

8

observed, and to find the right words with which to take others into his mind.

It was not to war, however, that the 1st North Staffs found themselves immediately transferred from County Cork, but to Cambridge and then Newmarket. It was a pleasant way to be fattened for the slaughter, with daily route-marches through the Cambridge countryside and dinner each night among the dons at the High Table of King's. As they returned from their exercises the youngest officer in the Battalion used to look out for a little girl who always rushed out of her house as they tramped by and sang them past to 'Marching through Georgia'. (When long years afterwards the battalion came home from France, that youngest officer, Vyvyan Pope, who by now had commanded the 1st North Staffs, arranged for it to be played back to barracks with the same march.)

But on 8 September they were on their way to Armageddon—in a cattle ship. Pope proceeded to his unknown destination armed with Shaw's *Plays Pleasant and Unpleasant*, an anthology of war poetry and a copy of *The Shropshire Lad*. As the Battalion foot-slogged up to the Aisne, it rained all the way.

CHAPTER TWO

A SEASON IN HELL

'La guerre, mon vieux, c'est notre jeunesse, ensevelie
et secrète.'
Henri de Montherlant, *Chant funèbre pour les morts
de Verdun.*

The legendary days of Mons and the Marne were
already over when, on the night of 21 September, the
Battalion crossed the Aisne and bivouacked in a sodden
cornfield. Pope and his unit had arrived during that brief
period of probing and re-adjustment before the British
and German armies sought to out-flank one another in the
'race to the sea' and trench warfare then imposed its
universal stranglehold. But it was a useful time for learning—learning, for example, that the sinister 'Jack Johnsons'
were not dangerous shells if one took precautions: that
the characteristic setting for Armageddon seemed to be a
drowned trench stinking of dead cow; that the Germans
were not just a race of waiters and bandsmen, but men
who could shoot straight. 'We also discovered that they
had Very lights, things of which we had never before
heard, and sandbags in abundance, whereas we had few
or none. Apparently they did know something about war.'
Pope was voicing his own early realization of an awkward
truth which was soon evident to all the BEF. In the early
days of manoeuvre the special skills of the Regular Army,
fast and accurate musketry, field craft, the best cavalry

in the world, had proved their superiority but were now of little value in the static siege warfare of the trenches. This would be a *materialenschlacht*, a war of equipment. Pope and his companions were ill-equipped: few or no machine-guns or hand-grenades or signal pistols, no heavy artillery, little and poor ammunition, nothing like a trench mortar. The BEF's loss of its virginity was therefore very painful.

There were other things to discover. 'I disgraced myself on my first spell of night-duty by refusing to wake up when my time came, and Charles Lyon had to walk me about for ten minutes before he was satisfied that I was at last awake. Whether his admonitions riddled my subconscious mind, or whether the mere fact of war once realized was never forgotten I do not know; but ever since that September night I have always been absolutely and fully awake immediately I am called.' By the end of the year, in fact, Pope and the North Staffs had learned the basic grammar of trench warfare. From the Aisne they were moved up into the Ypres sector and shared the rigours of that winter battle in which the Old Army, by holding off the determined German offensive, made the remainder of the war possible and maimed itself in the process. Pope's Battalion was not exceptionally engaged, yet by the end of 1914 it had lost 50% of its officers and nearly 50% of its men in killed and wounded, as well as many casualties from sickness.

On 16 December the Battalion had taken over trenches in the Rue du Bois area, charmingly known as 'Death Trap' or 'Dead Man's Alley', where life was spent more than knee-deep in mud and water and all reliefs had to be caried out in the open. It was here that they took part in the historic 'Christmas truce'. Pope was a principal negotiator. After the stand-down on Christmas Eve his Company Sergeant-Major asked him, 'What am I to do, Sir?

The Germans are sitting on their parapet, lighting candles and singing hymns'. Pope decided to enter no-man's-land and investigate.

'I found an affable German who had been a waiter in Brighton and wanted to tell me all about it, but cutting him short, I bade him lead me to his officer. He took me over to their front line where I found a group standing by the wall of a ruined farm-house. At first they were very suspicious and kept on asking me if I were armed. I was not and said so. "Word of a gentleman?" "Word of a gentleman", I solemnly replied. This appeared to relieve their minds and after an exchange of greetings I broached the matter uppermost in my mind: if we did not fire on them, would they not fire on us throughout Christmas Day? They affably agreed; and we established a truce forthwith till midnight German time which was an hour later than ours. Then I remembered that I could not stop our artillery firing, though in fact they seldom did fire for they had little or no ammunition and none to waste. I therefore said that I could not answer for the artillery, to which they replied that nobody could answer for them, they were a law unto themselves and no friend to the infantry. This seemed to be the proper spirit and I thought all was going well when a German asked permission to bury their dead which were thick in no-man's-land. In principle I was all for this since the dead were very dead and would be an extreme annoyance when the thaw came, but, as a junior Second-Lieutenant, I therefore said that I must consult a senior officer and after much friendly salutation went back to ask Jake Armes. He was delighted with the idea and quickly agreed to each side burying their dead in their own half of no-man's-land, starting at 10 am on Christmas Day.

'At 10 o'clock the following morning the burial parties went out from either side; at 10.10 the inevitable corpse was found astride the half-way line, and at 10.15 both parties were mingled in friendly disorder, exchanging souvenirs and swapping bully beef for cigars. I took several photographs of this scene, including one of a group of German officers who appeared so beautifully dressed that it was incredible that they could have set foot in their trenches. Amongst them were some Uhlans who had transferred to the infantry. They were all very friendly and warned us against the Prussians on our right who, they remarked, were not to be trusted. I was amused and yet horrified to observe one German officer chatting away with his foot negligently resting on the dead body of one of his men; they certainly had "the food for powder" spirit deeply imbued in them.'

The truce continued beyond Christmas, in a very un-official way. Indeed the Leinsters, who relieved the 1st North Staffs on 31 December, maintained this local attitude of good will to all men for many weeks, using the opportunity to improve their trenches. 'Rumour had it,' Pope remarked, 'that they exchanged barbed wire for stakes and that between them the British and the Germans wired no-man's-land almost solid.' But it was too good to last. GHQ sent up a staff officer to reconnoitre, and in consequence the Brigade Commander went home. 'Not peace, but a sword' was the motto for 1915.

Pope came of age as a front-line soldier during the night of 11/12 March, in the midst of the murderous battle of Neuve Chapelle—from which, for example, the 2nd Scottish Rifles emerged with one Second-Lieutenant in command, one Regimental Sergeant-Major and 143 men, having lost some 500 killed and wounded. The North Staffs were not directly involved, but their Brigade had been ordered to do what it could to prevent the transfer of German reinforcements to the main front. The Brigadier decided to capture and hold a small hamlet called L'Epinette, and young Pope, now commanding a company, played a distinguished part in repelling the inevitable counter-attack. He drove the company mercilessly, cursing a sergeant for leaving his platoon leaderless to sit by his dying officer, hectoring his exhausted men into wakefulness, meticulous in command. At a long day's end 'I was very anxious to get the wounded away as soon as it was safe to move under cover of darkness, but at the same time I dared not let too many go lest the Germans should repeat their bombing attack of the previous night. I therefore went along the line warning platoon commanders that only the most serious cases could go before we were relieved. No. 12 platoon's trench was a shambles and as I gave my orders to Lance-Corporal Proctor, the senior surviving NCO, my eyes fell upon Pte Lakin who had been so severely wounded in his shoulder that his arm appeared to be hanging on only by a thread. I was so shocked by the sight that I stopped in the middle of a sentence, but Lakin said "Don't you bother, Sir. We'll stick it all right"; and they did.'

For this action Pope received an immediate award of the Military Cross, the Battalion was praised by the Army Commander, and the capture of L'Epinette was mentioned by Kitchener in the House of Lords. The cost to the Battalion was seven officers and 124 other ranks killed and wounded.* Pope's chief satisfaction was the fact that he was able to obtain for Lance-Corporal Proctor promotion for gallantry in the field. 'That stalwart, illiterate ruffian had risen from company sanitary man to platoon sergeant

---

* This and other references to casualties take significance from the War Establishment of an infantry battalion, 29 officers and 971 other ranks, of whom a proportion were normally not front-line soldiers.

in six months of war, and he proved himself to be one of the best fighting sergeants we had.'

Whenever possible Pope revealed those qualtities of audacity and courage which befitted the future tank commander. His favourite spare-time occupation in the trenches was to watch and wait for the chance to snipe an unwary German—even after he himself had received a bullet through his cap. That cap, incidentally, he lost one night while crawling over no-man's-land in search of a wounded fellow-officer. In June, by which time the Battalion had moved into the Ypres Salient, he had another narrow escape when the officer beside him was shot through the stomach and lived, for two days, in agony. 'From that time onwards I felt convinced that it would be my lot to be shot in the stomach, an end I terribly feared.' Not surprisingly, there came a night when he was out beyond the front line and was suddenly attacked by fever. When he inched his way back to the dug-out, 'I fell into a semi-delirious slumber in which Stapleton and I and a horrible dead man with blackened face and foam-whitened lips struggled up Hooge Hill to rescue Uncle Harper* who had been captured by the whole German Army.'

After some days in a rest camp Pope returned to find that the Battalion was about to be inspected by the Second Army Commander, General Plumer, who praised the Battalion warmly and then pointed out that in the latest attack they had not been assaulting troops but had followed-up. 'You need not therefore be disappointed.' he said, 'if decorations do not come your way this time. Your turn will come, for I will see to it that in the next attack, like Uriah the Hittite, you are placed in the forefront of the battle.'

* Harper, the Brigade Commander, became more widely known by his nick-name 'Uncle' when he took command of the famous 51st Highland Division.

Pope (who had recently been Mentioned in Despatches) was appalled at the psychology of these words, addressed to a battalion which by now contained only a weary handful of the thousand-odd officers and men who had sailed for France. In retrospect the promise seems even more extraordinary, since it is totally out of character. Men trembled to be sent to the butcher Gough's Army, but as Haig's Chief of Intelligence, Charteris, wrote: 'When a division is rattled for any reason, either because of very heavy casualties or because it thinks it has had unfair treatment, it is sent to the Second Army, and at once becomes happy as sandboys.' Plumer, with his apple cheeks, his pot belly, and his white hair and moustache, balancing like a robin on spindle legs, was the quintessence of the soldiers' general, trusted and beloved. He must have had an off-day with the North Staffs.

Soon afterwards, in October, Pope's Brigade was transferred to the 24th Division. This was a result of the Battle of Loos, after which it was decided to stiffen New Army divisions with regular Brigades—a necessary transfusion, for Pope found the 24th in lamentable condition. 'They had been sadly misused at Loos and were still in a wretched state of confusion, both mental and organic.' With these tyros, ignorant of trench warfare, the North Staffs remained in the Ypres Salient for the next two months. Pope had now become Adjutant, a job whose chief drawback consisted in having to accompany a Colonel devoted to touring his Battalion above ground in daylight and in full view of the enemy.

On 29 April, 1916, Pope experienced his first major gas-attack. The gas was chlorine, and it is worth noting that the Battalion lost 112 men; in a second attack on 17 June the score was two officers and 154 men gassed and three officers and fifty-two men killed and wounded—a quarter of the Battalion. One needs constantly to refresh one's memory with such figures so as never to forget the strain on survivors like Pope, who, month in and month out, saw their battalions dissolving beside them and constantly recreated for a new dissolution, particularly survivors who multiplied experiences like Pope's during the April attack, described by him in a passage which might come from Siegfried Sassoon:

'I jumped on to the parapet and saw in the light of numerous flares many spreading clouds of greenish-yellow gas creeping across no-man's-land towards us. I jumped down and put on my helmet, and there we stayed in the support trench listening to the heavy small-arms fire from our front line and the bursting of the German shells about us. Presently my eye-pieces clouded and I slipped up a hand to clean them; after I had done this once or twice it struck me that I ought to have let in at least a little gas each time, and I wondered if the cloud had passed. Our signallers had been issued with the latest respirator which had detachable goggles, and I told one of them to take off his goggles quickly to see if his eyes were affected by the presence of gas. They were not; so I took off my helmet and found the air pure. Scarcely had I done so when I heard bombing in the front line on my right. Filling my pockets with bombs, I made by way towards it. As I went I was told that the Germans had captured D3, a small salient which covered one of our mine-entrances. Climbing on to the top, I straddled the communication trench leading to D3 and started to bomb my way down it. As I threw my first bomb, someone passing jolted my leg and my bomb fell in the open a few feet away. It burst, and a piece hit me in the cheek. The confusion was great and I remembered that I did not know where our men were and that I might well start a fight with them instead of the raiders. So I decided to start from the other flank and made a detour, over the top of the hill, till I struck 'B' Company's line well on the right. Here I collected a small party consisting of 'B' Company together with an officer and some men of an East Surrey working party, and we set off to retake D3. We bombed our way without resistance until we reached the apex of the salient, when turning a sharp traverse I saw, in the momentary light of a flare, two Germans approaching us. I cried out, "Surrender!" and the East Surrey officer, Youngman, who was with me, shouted: "Yes!" There was no reply and I doubt whether I allowed time for one, for almost instantaneously I fired my revolver point-blank at the leading man. The light had faded, but there was a loud groan from the Germans who rapidly withdrew leaving a rifle, which I seized, behind them. Our stocks of bombs had now gone, and to follow the raiders up through the maze of trenches was not very easy. As we went on we came to a divergence, one way leading through overhead cover whilst the other kept to the open trench. I told a private of the East Surreys to take the former whilst I cleared the latter. Both were empty, but as I stepped out into the open trench again the East Surrey whipped round and seeing me emerging from the shadow in the light of a flare, cried out, "Who are you?" and fired point-blank. I felt the bullet sear my chest and I shouted, "You bloody fool, you've killed me!" Then, realizing that I was scarcely hurt, I added hastily, "No, you haven't. It's all right; carry on." But my friend had vanished in the darkness and discretion or modesty prevented him from ever making himself known again.'

For his gallantry in this operation Pope received the immediate award of the DSO to add to his MC. He was a fortunate man: in the classic way, a cigarette case had turned the deadly bullet away from his chest.

But now there was the Somme. The 24th Division was not used in the terrible opening weeks of the battle and it was not until September that the next major series of assaults occurred. Arriving at the beginning of August, the division therefore found itself in the choppy water between the crests of two great waves. Nevertheless, places like Guillemont and Delville Wood are names of horror imprinted in the British racial memory, and Pope's Battalion attacked both. He knew now what was happening to him. 'The last party of the West Kents left and as it went a salvo of heavies came over and burst in their direction. I heard a scream, followed by groans. My morale by now was low, and I did not want to leave my trench, but I could not listen and do nothing; so I slipped out and found that a man had been horribly wounded but that Whitty of the West Kents was taking him away. As I ran back I realized that for the first time I had had to make a real and conscious effort to leave cover, and I knew my nerve was going!' This knowledge—or perhaps the fear that it *might* be true, stayed with him to the end. Summing up his four weeks on the Somme—during which 1st North Staffs lost sixteen officers and 374 men killed, wounded, and missing—Pope decided 'for myself, the war was henceforth always to be an effort; I had to will myself to do things which, however dangerous, must be done. In the past the necessity had clearly outweighed the danger, but in future I would balance both carefully and it would be with reluctance that I should see necessity bear down the scales.'

All the same, even though his morale might be slipping his moral courage was firm. During the attack on Guillemont two battalions in turn had failed to take a sunken road, to the south of the village, which was defended by machine guns in an impregnable pill-box. After the futile morning and afternoon attacks the Brigadier proposed to send in the North Staffs in the evening. Pope (as Adjutant) and his Colonel received these orders at Brigade HQ, and Pope believed that his Brigadier had lost all sense of reality. Young and junior though he was, he could endure the folly no longer and insubordinately protested. He won his point, the attack was postponed and then cancelled, and soon afterwards the Brigadier was relieved of his command. It requires an act of intense historical imagination to recapture the ethos of the pre-1914 Regular Army and to realise what daring—or perhaps what desperation —lay behind Pope's fortunate indiscipline.

At the end of October there was a move north to the Hulluch area, where the battalion remained for four months, and it was here that tanks first entered Pope's horizon. The sector was dull and Pope was restless: more to the point, his Colonel was lazy and suffered from chronic indigestion. He first applied for a transfer to the Royal Flying Corps, but nothing happened. Volunteers for the Tank Corps were also required. So far Pope had not seen tanks in action, but he put in for a transfer, was interviewed, and heard confidentially that he would be accepted. Then his Colonel informed him that his name could go forward as a potential staff officer, 'so I withdrew my application and remained an infantry soldier for another four years': and in February, 1917 he went off to the headquarters of the 72nd Brigade as a 'staff learner.'

The current Brigadier, Mitford, was a man of uncertain temper. He had recently visited Pope's Battalion and addressed the Colonel in soldierly language: 'Didn't I say that all helmets were to be covered with sandbags? And here you are with a painted abortion on your head looking like a bloody street-walker in the Edgware Road on a Saturday night. Get it covered at once, Sir, and tell that infernal doctor of yours that if he salutes me again with his pipe in his mouth I'll have him castrated.' However, he was shortly succeeded by the affable and easy-going Sweney, and for the next four months Pope's life was endurable.

But not without incident. When the Germans made a calculated withdrawal in April (as a result of the Vimy Ridge battle) Pope was typically up in the front line, personally taking prisoners and threatening with arrest a Royal Marine officer who seemed disposed to retire himself; and the next day, having obtained a roving commission from his Brigadier, he was back in no-man's-land—though a 'staff learner'—spontaneously organizing an attack on a German machine-gun position. It was the same on 7 June, the first day of the Battle of Messines. After the mines had exploded Pope was soon right forward on the furthermost infantry objective and—again typically—making the assault troops think him mad as he dashed about amid the mud and the dead, trying to finish off a hare he had wounded. 'For decency's sake', he wrote, 'I felt I must kill it.' Three days later he was up in the danger area again, when a bullet passed across his body and wounded him in the arm.

Things now moved quickly. Though a small nerve had been severed, he was only kept for a few days in the Casualty Clearing Station, and he was waiting to return to duty when he heard that the Colonel and Second-in-Command of the 1st North Staffs had been killed simultaneously by a shell. A few days later another shell killed the Colonel's successor. Brigadier Sweney therefore asked Pope to take over temporarily, as he was too young to be confirmed in command. Pope had just been offered a permanent staff job, but he naturally preferred his old unit, and not long afterwards was told that no suitable replacement could be found. So it was that Captain

Vyvyan Vavasour Pope, DSO, MC, at the age of twenty-five found himself an acting Lieutenant-Colonel in command of the Battalion which had been his family. It was no light task: 'The Battalion sorely needed a rest. During the month of June we had lost ten officers including two commanding officers, and we had nothing to show for it.' The Adjutant had lost his nerve. And it was the eve of Passchendaele.

At 3.50 am on 31 July the British barrage opened for the Third Battle of Ypres, and Pope discovered the loneliness and the agony of command. As he stood on the taped start-line watching his companies disappear in the dusky dawn and the smoke of German counter-fire, he had to repress his instinctive wish to be with them, and withdrew, instead, to his headquarter pill-box and the telephone. But no news or bad news from the front drew him out; and he managed to get across no-man's-land, where any movement now attracted shell or bullet, and to make contact with his men. Only two officers were left of the eleven who had set out, and the Battalion, enfiladed by machine-guns, had been slaughtered. (Of 530 other ranks who attacked, 258 were lost in two hours.) Rain now turned the pulverized soil into a muddy morass. Pope felt an intense misery, and bitter self-reproach. Could he have done better? Was he not unfit for command? But it was not the Battalion Commanders who were wrong at Passchendaele, and in fact the Divisional Commander called in person to make his congratulations.*

So Pope took the strain and endured the loneliness—even the worst, and inevitably solitary, decision, that of agreeing to the capital sentence on a persistent deserter and laying on the firing party for his execution.

* The Battalion had actually secured its objectives. The most advanced positions gained could not be maintained because of the failure of other units on each flank, which left the 1st North Staffs exposed.

During the rest of the year the North Staffs were continuously in or about the front line, though fortunately not deeply committed. It was now a matter of daily erosion by the sheer routine of the front—trench-raids, bombing from the air, the constant artillery. On 20 November they were on the right of the Cambrai battlefield, but though they expected to be drawn in as reserves to face the triumphant German counter-attack, their good fortune held. All the same, Pope recognized that 'I was now getting very stale and I was suffering from sleeplessness due partly to violent indigestion. To visit the line under the slightest fire had become a distinct effort, and the responsibility of command weighed upon me far more heavily than it should do.' The healthy subaltern of 1914 had been converted into a man who would suffer from gastric disorders for the rest of his life. The symptoms were becoming evident, for early in December his humane Brigadier suddenly rang and ordered him, in spite of expostulations, to get back home on a month's leave.

When Pope returned to the Battalion in the New Year he found Lieutenant-Colonel Wyatt in command. However, 'the Divisional Commander went out of his way personally to explain that had he not been on leave when Wyatt arrived, this would not have occurred.' In a few weeks, anyway, Wyatt departed to take over the 72nd Brigade and Pope once again led the 1st North Staffs—into the most appalling of all its wartime experiences.

They had moved south during the winter, to just north of St Quentin. It was on 15 March that Pope recovered command, and already the air was full of rumours of a coming German offensive. On the 17th the Battalion entered the front line and found itself in a situation so typical of the ill-fated Fifth Army. The trenches were indifferent, the wiring inadequate, the dug-outs meagre. The position had a frontage of 2,000 yards and a depth of 3,000, a huge area for a weak battalion to defend. (Pope had to hold 1,000 yards of front with a company, his headquarters and a machine-gun section). The 18th, 19th and 20th of March passed tranquilly, though Pope had an inner sense that trouble was coming—in spite of the optimism around him. But at 4.40 next morning all uncertainties were dispelled by the clamour of 6,608 enemy guns.

'I ran the twenty yards from my bunk to the signal office, but as I pulled back the blanket which screened the doorway the signaller on duty looked up and said, "All lines dissed, Sir". There was not a buried cable in the whole area. I went up to the trench. The night was still and dark and there was a heavy mist. I could see nothing, but I breathed deeply of gas before I realized that gas shells were falling about us. Our information, which had so far proved correct, was that the German bombardment would last some five hours, so beyond doubling our sentries I kept the men under cover. Then I went to my dug-out and destroyed all secret papers. I did not know what to do with my diary which contained a complete record of all our doings; I could not bring myself to destroy it, so reluctantly I hid it behind the skirting. Our canteen money I put in my haversack. Then I returned to the mess-room and waited. I felt very ill as a result of the gas I had inhaled.'

As dawn broke a subaltern of the Argyll and Sutherland Highlanders arrived to say his Battalion had moved up to fill a gap on Pope's right, though their Colonel had been killed even before they started. But the mist which had so favoured the Germans was still thick, and it was not until mid-morning that a twenty-yard visibility enabled Pope to inspect his nearest defences. The men were cool and confident, but there was no sign of the Argylls. Remembering the precept, 'Go and see for yourself', Pope set out to find them. Suddenly three figures loomed in the mist. A glance through field-glasses revealed the silhouette of a German helmet, so he immediately picked up his rifle and dropped the first intruder. But as the man fell, a second fired back at Pope and hit him on the right elbow while his arm was still bent in the act of shooting. The bone was shattered.

Nevertheless he escaped in the mist and, ironically, found himself among the Argylls whom he had been seeking. A Highlander helped him back to the rear, Pope having lashed his flapping arm to his side with his Sam Browne belt. Then the inevitable sequence began—Forward Dressing Station, Casualty Clearing Station Ambulance Train, Hospital, with the graph of pain steadily, and in the end intolerably, rising. At Rouen a physician and a surgeon examined him. 'The bandages were undone and I realized that my wound stank. The physician looked at me and then at the surgeon and said, "No doubt about that, I think." "You're going to take it off?" I asked. "Must, old man", he replied; and they had it off within twenty minutes. I had got gas gangrene.'

He became delirious. His resentments focused on a worthy Matron, about whose delinquencies he composed a long satirical poem which he immediately forgot. A chaplain tried to get him to take communion, on the assumption that he was dying, but he had not communicated for years and his belligerent spirit refused to allow him to do so on the off-chance of slinking into Heaven through the back door. Perhaps this was a sign of life, for he recovered quickly; indeed, within ten days of being wounded he wrote the first letter with his left hand.

But there was no quick release from pain. After he had been moved to the Swedish War Hospital in London other wounded survivors visited him, and from their stories he gradually pieced together what had happened on 21 March. The Battalion he commanded had been destroyed. When the remnants rallied shortly after midday, the total was two Second-Lieutenants and twenty-one other ranks. The Regimental Sergeant-Major had gone, killed as he wielded a rifle, declaring that he had been a marksman in 1901 and would show the buggers what a marksman could do. The former Adjutant recovered his nerve in death. A bomb burst on his shoulder and his servant ran to him. 'Don't bother about me', he cried. 'I'm done for anyway. Get on into the fight.' The new Adjutant, badly wounded in the head, attacked a German post with the bayonet; and the small headquarters group he led must have fought well, for when, months afterwards, a fellow-officer returned in a fruitless hunt for the papers Pope had concealed he found on the spot a cross commemorating twenty German soldiers who had died that day. During the whole war the Battalion's casualties were 126 officers and 3,872 other ranks: 21 March, 1918, was its greatest tragedy, and so it must particularly have seemed to its young Commanding Officer who had served with it from the start.

Nor was he finished with physical pain. Though his arm was healing well, the end of the bone separated and a fresh operation was necessary. 'That swine's broken me; I'm broken', he groaned as he came out of the anaesthetic. 'The nurse said "No, not broken: only a little bent." So I realized that I was being slightly ridiculous and stopped making so outrageous a fuss.' But at last he was off on three months' sick leave and then, armless, faced a Medical Board. 'What', said the President, 'would you do if you met a German face to face?' Pope argued that in fact his General wanted him back in France as ADC, but neither that ploy, nor his return a fortnight later wearing—for the only time in his life—a false arm had any success. However, hope dawned when he heard that the Commanding

Officer of the 1st North Staffs in France had been wounded, and had applied for him.

Eagerly he made his way to the War Office, to visit and cajole the Staff Officer responsible for postings. This divinity, however, waved all Pope's papers aside. 'I'm afraid it's no good now', he said. 'The Germans have signed and all postings to France are cancelled.' The day was 11 November, 1918.

CHAPTER THREE

RUSSIAN ROULETTE

'A man who gives himself to be the possession of aliens leads a Yahoo life, having bartered his soul to a brute-master. He is not of them. He may stand against them, persuade himself of a mission, batter and twist them into something which they, of their own accord, would not have been. Then he is exploiting his old environment to press them out of theirs.'

T. E. Lawrence, *Seven Pillars of Wisdom*

Some time after 1945 Churchill observed to his medical adviser, Lord Moran, 'Don't you feel lonely without a war? I do.' Once the immediate relief of an armistice had been savoured, this was a feeling shared in 1919 by many combatant soldiers on both sides. The more extreme elements naturally found extreme ways of expressing their frustration—the *Freikorps* in Germany, the Black and Tans in Ireland. But in an entirely legitimate and understanding way even responsible and well-balanced men like Pope were dogged by a sense of anticlimax. Battle had made the adrenalin flow, but there was little to stimulate in the conditions of peacetime England.

This was particularly a problem for the professional soldier. Others might return to established civilian careers or enjoy the excitement of carving out a new life. But for regular officers like Pope war was the rationale of the career to which they had committed themselves when they received the King's Commission, and during the last four years the Germans had given them a unique opportunity to exercise their professional skills. To command a battalion in one's mid-twenties, to be twice decorated in the field for courage, to have fought in every major battle, to have been seriously wounded and have survived—such intense experiences could hardly be compensated for by the sedate and uninspiring routine of a regimental depot in some drab provincial town. And there was something else. For the last four years Pope had been inhabiting a world which had disappeared overnight. All who have become citizens of the front line in any war know that it is a civilization, a culture, a community with its own laws, its own code of conduct, its own atmosphere: a foreign land to all but its colonists—and for them it is home. By comparison the so-called Home Country, England, seemed curiously alien to men like Pope at the beginning of 1919. No wonder he wrote of 'the boredom of a peaceful world in which we felt out of place and unwanted'.

Certainly the Repatriation Camp at Winchester was an unattractive haven. Here men from the Dominions and Colonies who had enlisted in the British Army were being assembled before returning to their own countries, and hither Pope was sent to take over a company. A 'company', he discovered on arrival, consisted of over 1,000 men on the verge of mutiny. (This was a genuine possibility. Dilatory mismanagement of an unimaginative scheme for demobilization produced several such outbreaks—at Folkestone and Calais, for example, at Glasgow and Belfast. The 'Father of the RAF', Trenchard, had to use draconian measures at Southampton to bring to order 20,000 rebellious servicemen.) 'No orders were given, only requests; no parades were held, but it was suggested occasionally that for exercise the men might like to take a walk together;

officers and NCOs generally exchanged salutes, but otherwise the practice was abandoned; any government property that was saleable was freely sold, and blankets were scarcely negotiable in Winchester.' After his spirited and well-disciplined battalion Pope loathed the atmosphere of a place where the staff were terrified of the men, and the men were bored by enforced idleness.

But relief came unexpectedly soon. He sent a cry for help to an old friend at the War Office, and was summoned to be interviewed for a staff job. This in itself was not propitious. ' "And what was your school?" asked the spruce colonel. I felt that to obtain Honours the required answer was Eton or Harrow, and that Winchester might just scrape pass-marks, so it was with some trepidation that I murmured "Lancing". "Ah yes", he replied with the vague politeness of a man who feels that unsuspectingly he has asked an indelicate question.' A few days later, oddly enough, he was informed that the post for which he had applied had been abolished. However, he returned to the attack, and visited Whitehall again to press another application—for permission to join the Russian Relief Force. On the doorstep of the War Office he met by chance the commander of one of the two Brigades being formed to go to Russia. They were not acquainted, but Pope immediately tackled him, was taken inside, and as a result obtained a vague appointment on the Embarkation Staff. This he readily accepted, having decided that as soon as he got to Russia he would give the Staff the slip and join a fighting unit.

If the cards were stacked against Pope and his Battalion when with high hearts they landed in France in 1914, still more was this true of the Russian Relief Force. British intervention on the side of the Whites had been substantial —some £100,000,000 in war material, volunteers with Kolchak in Siberia and Denikin in the south, an occupation force at Baku, and conglomerates at Archangel and Murmansk which served the double purpose of aiding the Whites and guarding the huge dumps of ammunition delivered there by Great Britain during the war. But if these and other efforts had ever achieved anything more than to confirm the new rulers of Russia in their obsessive distrust of capitalism, they had lost their validity by the spring of 1919. Increasing disaffection among the White Russian units, the ever-growing menace of the Bolsheviks and, in Great Britain itself, a spreading distaste for the whole venture all combined to impress on the Cabinet the need for a favourite British manoeuvre—evacuation. The name of the Russian Relief Force told its own tale. It was not created to win victories but to cover a retreat.

Such, however, were not the thoughts in the minds of Pope and his fellow-passengers on His Majesty's Temporary Transport *Czaritza*, (a small, unseaworthy, ex-Russian ship) as they rolled and lurched on their week-long voyage from Newcastle to Murmansk. Their outlook was rosier. 'We were a strange collection of adventurers drawn from every arm and regiment, and I could not but pity in anticipation the innocent Bolsheviks when we should be loosed among them. Many of us, I suspected, found His Majesty a better paymaster than we were likely to achieve elsewhere, and some of us certainly had hopes of bartering bottles of whisky for the richest furs and boxes of chocolates for the favours of beautiful women. A few, like myself, were seeking relief from the boredom of a peaceful world in which we felt out of place and unwanted.'

When *Czaritza* reached Archangel Pope immediately set about dissociating himself from the Embarkation Staff. An amiable GSO 2 said that he might have something more active for him, and within a few days that something emerged. It was a proposition typical of the freebooting character who was in command of this miscellany of freebooters, 'Tiny' Ironside, the youngest Major-General in the British Army. By character and ability Ironside, who had arrived in September, 1918, as Chief of Staff and now was master, had organized a heterogeneous collection of many nationalities into something like a coherent army. His later failure as CIGS, a post for which he knew he was not equipped, should not be allowed to blur his achievement in North Russia, which few could have surpassed.

Ironside had recently visited the Archangel prison and been horrified to discover that many of its inhabitants were in gaol either for very minor offences or often without any charge at all being preferred against them. Some men were behind bars simply because nobody knew what to do with them. It was all very Russian. The General was convinced that good material was going to waste and he was determined to make use of it. Another mixed Slavo-British battalion would be a mistake, as this would be a further charge on the British Government. He therefore proposed to form a unit composed entirely of ex-prisoners, for which the Russians would pay, and to put a British officer in command. This was the attractive proposition laid before Pope. Would he take it on? He said he would, and next day was interviewed by Ironside.

'He told me that my men would come with charges of Bolshevism, mutiny, murder, theft and lesser offences hanging over them, but that I was not to take such charges too seriously.' He believed that regular food, regular pay, careful handling, and above all exhaustion by hard work might turn them into admirable soldiers. Perhaps conscious of Pope's missing arm, he asked whether he could tackle the job. With Neuve Chapelle, Ypres, the Somme, Passchendaele and the March, 1918 battle behind him, Pope simply replied with some austerity that he had commanded a battalion in France. 'Yes, yes', said Tiny, 'but this is a very different business'. In the event, Pope was appointed and received from Ironside a liberal charter. 'Treat them as a British officer treats his men and they will do anything for you, but if you have trouble hit hard. You can do what you like in the way of punishment but unless things are very bad you had better not shoot anybody or use the cat without reference to me.' Wide though his terms of reference sounded, the Commander of the new Russian Disciplinary Company was going to need their full scope.

Among Pope's papers there is a type-written document, yellow with age, entitled 'General organization and instructions for the administration of a Russian Disciplinary Company, based on an initial strength of 100 Rank and File'. The orderly paragraphs and formal presentation give it an air of *fait accompli*. The Company Commander was to be British, with a staff of one subaltern, a Company Sergeant-Major and one Sergeant to act as Company Quartermaster-Sergeant. The rest would be Russians. A training programme follows, and details about canteens, messes and so on. 'To begin with half rates of pay will be issued, and then the rates will be gradually increased as each individual appears to be reformed'. An Appendix 'B' set out a scale of equipment: Knives carving 4, Plates 266, Mops 3 etc. Perhaps the item least useful for the Commander of this unusual unit was to be found under the heading 'Miscellaneous':—soft soap.

For Archangel, of course, was not quite like Aldershot. 'I now', wrote Pope, 'came up against that blank wall of passive obstruction with which the Orient seeks to ward off the insect-like activity of the European and behind which the European so easily takes refuge in an Oriental country.' The camp was full of idle soldiery, but he could not raise his British staff; the town was full of plates, but he could not get an issue. Finally the threat of a direct appeal to Ironside made things move, and even produced an interpreter—whose arrival was closely followed by letters stating: '*re* Private Bologovsky, this man must be watched and must not be entrusted with confidential work of any kind', and 'This man must not be given any money and not be entrusted with money affairs of any kind'. He was, unfortunately, Pope's sole means of communication with his men.

A barracks was found for the Company in the shape of ten log huts in a forest clearing, some distance down the railway to Archangel and suitably called Tundra. On 6 June the unit formally began its life—and the dossiers rolled in. 'A man told a militiaman...', 'he is said to have...', 'they think that...' were the typical reasons for the men's imprisonment. Pope therefore decided to take a calculated risk, and on parade next morning he told the Company that the past was dead. 'They received this oration with soldierly immobility, but they carried out the long day's work I imposed on them without a murmur.' Improvization was inevitable. An ex-tinsmith carved mugs out of bully beef tins, and as there were no cap-badges Pope arranged for the six-pointed star of his family crest to be cut out of the white metal of ration biscuit-tins. Few men had socks.

The future seemed set fair. All property removed from the men in gaol was extorted from a reluctant Prison Governor, and Pope appalled the Russian authorities, while no doubt astonishing his troops, by insisting that his Company should be paid the correct amount each week. One evening after parade Bologovsky presented his Commanding Officer with a 'petition' on behalf of all ranks. 'Sir, we have arrived up here and have the reputation of criminals we all have seen carefully and with human respect. We all ar much obliged to you, Sir, for having arranged such nice games like music, books, chess etc. Olso we thank you, Sir, for to try and find out and improve our situation as citizens in the society and in the Empire, because at present our situation put us in a class of people for which the doors of society are closed. Once more we all thank you, Sir, for all your car and we hope that by our good faith and work your respect to us will be careful and humane.'

Encouraged by these signs of good will Pope now obtained a stock of rifles and began serious tactical training and musketry exercises. But the first sign that his idyll could not last came when he received another draft of 106 men. These had been sent straight from Russian battalions at the front, and were all distrusted or thought to be dangerous by their commanding officers. Nevertheless they disapproved of Pope's gaol-birds, and he therefore formed from them a second company, rechristening his unit the Russian Disciplinary Battalion. With firm and careful handling, and a judicious issue of leave-passes into Archangel, the mixture seemed to be settling down: indeed, on 7 July another 'petition' was submitted, this time for a concert stage, which declared: 'You can be positive, Sir, its our best wishes to absolutely obey all your orders and if anyone from us will be a bad man against of your orders all we will make him do and satisfied you and all your officer under your gently command.' That seemed clear enough. 'Surely at least the elements of loyalty were taking root amongst the men', Pope dared to imagine. 'In fact I thought I was turning them into willing soldiers whom I could hopefully lead into action. That was indeed my chief desire, and it seemed to me that it might soon be fulfilled—but I was dreaming.'

The men had no intention of becoming front-line soldiers. This became evident on 16 July, when Pope received an urgent telephone call in the early hours of the morning ordering him to disarm his troops immediately. Several Slavo-British battalions had mutinied and shot some

British officers. Pope therefore held his usual morning parade and told the men that he had been instructed to return their arms but that he proposed to get the order rescinded as soon as possible. In the evening he addressed them again, telling them of his confidence in them. 'Then I made my crowning error.' He had long been hoping, he said, that the General would let them go as a fighting unit to the front. He intended to ask for the return of their arms to equip them for battle, but wished to be able to tell the General that the Russian Disciplinary Battalion had volunteered for this service. With little hesitation the whole unit took one pace forward 'I was delighted; but I had wrecked the Battalion.' There were four desertions that night, and four more the next day.

In a larger sense all Pope's concern was irrelevant, since for the British, and indeed for the Whites, the tides were already running out on the North Russian front. But he was young, he was professional, he was proud; the command he had been given was virtually unmanageable, and he was determined to manage it. As soon as he began to investigate the desertions, however, he discovered he had misinterpreted the situation. When he tackled the local stationmaster the truth emerged. ' "Why", he said, "didn't you know? They're going to kill you." I explained that they had neglected to inform me of their purpose. "Oh yes", he said, "it's all fixed up. I thought you knew all about it: it's common knowledge in the village." '

The mere threat of murder left Pope unshaken. He had always moved weaponless among his criminals, and they could have killed him at any time; the disarming parade would have been a perfect opportunity. Far more disconcerting was the probability of mass desertion. He immediately rang up GHQ in Archangel and ordered a special train. By the following evening he was back in Tundra with a VC, Captain Batten-Pooll, and twenty Royal

Fusiliers. So supported he ordered all his Russians to their barracks, proclaimed a curfew, posted sentries on the huts and patrols round the village, and told them to shoot without hesitation at anybody who failed to answer the password.

This, though good for one night, was hardly a long-term solution. How could he impede or even prevent further desertion? He suddenly remembered that he had heard of Pathan prisoners in India being stopped from running away by the removal of their pyjama-strings. Well, he could hardly impound his men's trousers, but he could take away their boots, and with good reason; the nearest village was thirty miles away and the local terrain was not kind to bare feet. The next morning, therefore, half an hour before reveille when spirits are at their lowest, he fell in the Battalion hut by hut and had the men marched to the Quartermaster's stores to hand in their boots while he searched their kit. He found no hidden arms, but did bring to light a small stock of rifle ammunition, and also discovered that most of the men had built up a reserve of at least two days' supply of ration biscuit.

That evening a Military Control Officer arrived, and the next few days were filled with arresting and interrogating suspects, including the egregious Bologovsky whom Pope sent off to his fate with a plea in mitigation. As a result Bologovsky was only imprisoned, while his clerk was shot—one of the three prisoners executed out of the thirteen Pope handed over to the White Russians. Then, on the 21st, he heard that two of his deserters had been arrested at a village thirty miles away, having walked there down the railway, barefoot, in twenty-four hours. By now Pope had already informed GHQ that he could no longer hold the Battalion together at its detached outpost; searches had revealed that women were coming in by train carrying seditious papers, and the mood at Tundra was rapidly deteriorating. He therefore demanded the immediate return of the deserters and rang up Archangel to say he wanted to shoot them. Ironside's permission and the deserters—and orders to move the Battalion forthwith—all arrived the next day.

Pope made the Russians themselves carry out the execution. One of the deserters died shouting 'Hurrah for the Bolsheviks and long live the Russian Republic!' After the shots rang out, 'The two bodies hung in the air', Pope noted, 'as though time and gravitation and all natural seemly things had been suspended; then they dropped together on the earth.' The Russians' aim had been poor: one of the pair was wounded in the head, and the other, hit in the lungs, brought up white-bubbled blood with each stertorous breath. Pope put them at peace with a revolver bullet through the heart. 'I had executed two men because rule by fear was now the only way in which I could maintain discipline, but I despised myself for having to do it; rule by fear was a sorry substitute for the rule by trust and confidence which I had hoped, and failed, to establish.' A Yahoo life, T. E. Lawrence had called his existence among the Arabs: and this experience of Pope's is curiously reminiscent of the passage in the *Seven Pillars* in which Lawrence describes how, to avoid a blood feud among his men, he had to execute one of them himself, alone, with his revolver, and there 'rose up that horror which would make civilized man shun justice like a plague if he had not the needy to serve him as hangmen for wages'.

He had thought it possible that one of the firing-party might have saved a bullet for his Commanding Officer, but all was well, and indeed the Battalion packed up its baggage and entrained that night without demur. Its destination, however, was no improvement on Tundra, for when they reached Archangel they were taken by barge to an island some way to the north, Economia. The only means of getting to the city was by water or by a long walk down the defunct railway, and the only significant thing about Economia was the hundreds of thousands of shells stacked in the sheds along the wharves. These had been shipped by the Allies for onward passage to Rumania and had been cut off by the Russian Revolution. It was a wild and desolate spot, surrounded by marshes and mud, but throughout August Pope kept his Battalion docile, improving their living conditions and working them hard at loading ammunition into barges for dumping out at sea—the final stages of the evacuation being imminent.

For this the most complicated plans were drawn up, in case White Russian control collapsed. In that event Pope's own task would certainly have been complicated, for he was charged with a unique command consisting of a destroyer, an armoured train and a section of tanks! However, he was never called on to carry out this amphibious operation; his most delicate problem was to certify that certain Russians, having aided the Allied cause, were in danger of losing their lives if they were not evacuated. This became delicate indeed when the Assistant Base Commandant pleaded with Pope to certify his pregnant mistress. Pope sent for her and explained that as he did not know her he could not very well sign the certificate unless she were prepared to do something for him. She looked at Pope with liquid eyes of surrender and made a passionate statement. 'She says', the interpreter translated impartially, 'that she will do anything in the world for your Honour.' 'Then will you ask her to darn these socks?'

On 24 September Pope paraded the Disciplinary Battalion for the last time, before handing it over to the White Russian Command. The men listened to his farewell address in silence, but he felt their reproach. When he said that those who were loyal had nothing to fear, reproach changed to scornful incredulity. And this, he knew in his heart, was justified. He knew that their next commanders would imprison those they did not immediately shoot; before Archangel was inevitably abandoned to the Bolsheviks even the survivors would be eliminated. He felt, too, an oppressive sense of failure. Of his 197 men five had been executed, twelve had been arrested and fourteen had deserted. He embarked with relief on the *Czar*, the last vessel to leave Archangel, and as the ship slipped down the river he looked for the last time at Economia and the bare flagstaff where, to the fury of the Russians, he had flown a Battalion banner of his own design.

CHAPTER FOUR

IRISH JIG

'Those fanatics all that we do would undo;
Down the fanatic, down the clown;
Down, down, hammer them down,
Down to the tune of O'Donnell Abu.'
W. B. Yeats, *Three Songs to the Same Tune*

Pope's main companion on the *Czar* was Dostoievsky's *The Idiot*. This was perhaps as relevant reading for one about to enter the Ireland of the IRA as it was for one departing from Bolshevised Russia. For after some leave he was posted back to the 1st Battalion of the North Staffs, which was stationed at the Curragh.

Here was a Slough of Despond worse than Archangel. Pope had naively supposed that he would find his old unit more or less the same as it was in 1914, but of course he was deluded. Like so many battalions in the immediate post-war period, the 1st North was at a low ebb: a medley of officers widely separated by age and experience, and troops (on short service enlistment) who were either idle or incompetent or runaways from civil life. In the Officers' Mess there were either senior pre-war antiquities, or a few young survivors like Pope, and the odd 'temporary commission'. For those annealed in the front line there was little communication with the Boer War mentality of the elders or the innocence of their juniors.

Moreover, the characters of his fellow-officers were

unattractive. One was the Second-in-Command, flashing his double row of medals. 'He commanded respectful admiration at first sight. Unfortunately he did not command it long and he was quite incapable of commanding anything else ... certainly he was far more successful in the active service of Venus than he had ever been in that of Mars.' There was the alcoholic Major who appeared speechless with drink before the parade of men he was due to march off as a draft to Egypt. Next morning a telegram arrived: 'All records and documents destroyed by fire. All ranks wish you a happy Christmas.' (The soldiers to whom he had unwisely entrusted the draft's papers had themselves got drunk and made a bonfire of the lot.) There was the inhuman Adjutant who had only served in West Africa and the other Major who, with great skill, had contrived to be *embusqué* since August, 1914. Pope called them 'the flotsam and the jetsam of a great war'. He was rescued by becoming the temporary Brigade Major of the Curragh Brigade.

Throughout 1920 the tempo of violence in Ireland increased steadily as the British added to their 50,000 troops and 10,000 Royal Irish Constabulary the Black and Tans, and then the Auxiliaries, each of whom answered with terror the terrorism of Sinn Fein and the IRA. Apart from these special units, neither the army nor the police had either the mentality or the training for guerrilla war. Moreover, as in Ulster in the 1970s, the problem of preserving law and order was insoluble so long as the lawbreakers could melt into the cover of a sympathetic population. And this, inevitably, was Pope's experience. During the early part of 1920 the rebels around Dublin were concentrating on the murder of policemen, and the commander of Pope's division considered that 'aid to the civil power' was less important than the essential task of training his raw soldiers.

Nevertheless, occasionally attempts were made to round up an assassin. A typical pattern would begin with a call to Brigade HQ from the Divisional Police Inspector asking for troops to be sent to a small town thirty miles away where the police sergeant had been shot and all telephone wires cut. Pope would order out a detachment under an officer. All would be quiet when they arrived, except the nerves of the police. The sergeant, they would learn, had been shot when opening the door at his usual time to take in the evening paper. And that was all they would learn.

It was this doldrum period, nevertheless, which started Pope off on a journey into a new world. He was still Brigade Major when two letters arrived in the office, one asking for Territorial Army adjutants and the other for volunteers for the Tank Corps. Pope applied, and was accepted, for both employments. On balance, he thought the tanks would be more interesting. The critical fact, however, was his new determination to get to the Staff College, and for this the Tank Corps looked a better launching pad. It was thus entirely in a spirit of opportunism that he became one of that second vintage of officers who, after its wartime birth and post-war decline, would re-vivify in Great Britain the 'armoured idea'.

Pope arrived at Wareham early in April, 1920—and almost immediately returned to Ireland. The 19th Tank Battalion to which he had been posted was in process of absorption by the 4th Battalion. His keen professional mind was not impressed by what he saw. 'I had fled from dull, gentlemanly and inefficient stagnation; here I found a confused and riotous vortex out of which might emerge anything.'

The situation was that five Armoured Car Companies were being formed, to be officered entirely by volunteers drawn from other arms and seconded to the Tank Corps, a process looked on with disdain by those who had served in armour during the war. In Pope's view, many of the 'volunteers' had been discreetly detached from their regiments for their regiments' good. Rounds of drinks started in the Mess at 11 am and continued until midnight. Pope was neither a prig nor a puritan, but he was a wholly dedicated soldier and this was not the way to run an army.

Of the five companies two were due to go to Iraq and two to Egypt. The fifth was to be formed in Dublin from the 17th Tank Battalion. After four years of France and a bout in Russia Pope opted for Ireland. He had not yet been sufficiently close to the terrorism and counter-terrorism to be deterred by the idea of returning. It was the company he had had to keep which had repelled him.

Nor, indeed, did he find Dublin in May, 1920, an unattractive city. 'The troubles' still mainly affected the police. Indeed, it was typical of the Pope who read Dostoievsky as he lurched over the North Sea from Russia that, because of a growing interest in the work and life of William Blake, one of the first things he did was to seek out the Irish poet and sage 'AE', George Russell. Unfortunately he was introduced as one ignorant of the poet's King Charles's Head—the Irish Agricultural Board —and, as Pope put it, 'the barque of our conversation was launched upon a slipway from which there was no escape'. Instead of Blake, therefore, 'AE' applied himself with his characteristic amalgam of mysticism and common sense to the mundane problems of agricultural economics, and, being an Irishman, to politics. 'When the Universe was resolved into its primal elements,' he said, 'and reabsorbed into the Godhead, Ulster would be found drafting Solemn Covenants reiterating her determination never to surrender her unique and splendid identity by fusion with any other power whatsoever'—a long-term forecast certainly supported by the next half-century.

In spite of 'AE's vivid and witty conversation, poured out over the rising mountain of burnt matches which fed his unsmoked pipe, Pope nevertheless said farewell to him with a sense of unease. 'If so great a man', he thought, 'who strove so manifestly to be impartial in his judgements could not wholly force himself from the Irishman's heritage of hate for England, and England was the enemy throughout his talk, what hope was there of the unthinking masses throwing off that ancient heritage and how could we reconcile cold-blooded murder and furtive assassination with these high ideals!' As he settled in with his new unit, of which he was Second-in-Command, he began to realize from experience the impossibility of answering his own question.

The unit itself was well-officered and efficient, and its commander was Douglas Pratt, one of the stalwarts of British armour, for as a Major he had led a tank company into the Battle of Cambrai in 1917, and as a Brigadier he would command the only brigade of tanks with the British Expeditionary Force in France when the Germans struck in 1940.

But what of 'the unthinking masses'? A one-day general strike was proclaimed in Dublin as a demonstration against the imprisonment of the Lord Mayor of Cork, who was on hunger-strike. Some of the Company's heavy tanks and armoured cars were sent down to the prison to assist the infantry in keeping a large crowd away from the gates. Pope went to see what was happening. The crowd was restive, alternating between listening to exhortations not to interfere with the military and kneeling down, rosary in hand, for the occasional prayer. 'The infantry were mere youths, untrained and unhappy, and they were being subjected to verbal abuse by a few unruly women, which they resented. Their rifles were loaded and behind them were the loaded 6-pounder guns and machine-guns of the tanks and armoured cars. A young and bewildered infantry captain was in charge. I walked round the cordons and saw one old woman smack an infantryman's face: she was immediately removed by the Irish volunteers but the delighted crowd was scarcely held in hand.' On Pope's initiative a Staff Officer was immediately sent to take charge, but the vivid impression remained with him of how one small provocation, a single shot by a raw young soldier, and an uncontrollable reaction from the crowd could have led to massacre.

There was now no relaxation. He acquired a small car and spent his spare time exploring the Dublin countryside, but inevitably found himself one day face to face with an armed rebel. He coolly drove past—and on his return found that a patrol had flushed out a group of Sinn Feiners from the house the man was guarding.

More serious was the affair of the bank. It was Pope's practice to draw the weekly pay for the Company in an armoured car, carefully changing the halting place and the hour of arrival every Friday. One afternoon, however, he noticed as he dismounted that the usual line of 'side-cars' awaiting hire was missing from the middle of the street, though there was the customary knot of corner-boys grinning at him as he entered the bank. Suddenly, as he reached the counter, a machine-gun stuttered and window-glass rained down. When he went to the door to investigate one of the corner-boys put a pistol to his head at point-blank range. The hammer fell: but there was no explosion. The street was now empty except for one groaning Sinn Feiner, whose head had been shattered by a bullet from the armoured car. In spite of protests from a gathering crowd Pope insisted on keeping the wounded man for identification, and refused to let him be moved until a military ambulance had arrived. When a fire brigade ambulance turned up first, Pope with apparent cruelty—as it seemed to the abusive Dubliners—still held back his prisoner, for he knew that if the fire brigade carried him away the man would vanish without trace. What he could not explain publicly was that he had seen far too many head wounds in recent years not to be certain that the Sinn Feiner was already to all intents and purposes dead.

The Dublin Command was afraid that Pope might be singled out for reprisal and cautiously issued a statement that the officer concerned had had his arm in a sling. But the Sinn Fein were quicker in their reaction, so that the evening papers carried a full description which deeply humiliated Pope by its claim that the armed men had spared his life because of his disability. As a result everybody knew who the one-armed officer was, and he started to be congratulated by strangers on his escape. His seniors therefore decided to send him to England for a week, to let things blow over. With that *panache* which came so naturally to him he insisted, before departing, on accompanying a special raiding party which tried, unsuccessfully, to catch in his hiding-place the hero of the Easter Rising and ringleader of the IRA, Michael Collins.

Courage is a variable commodity. Submariners shiver at the thought of being airmen, and airmen, in the First World War, would look down from their flimsy and too often perishable planes on to the infantry travailing in the mud and wonder how they could endure. Pope had kept his nerve on the Western Front, greatly though it had been tested. But he was frank with himself about his visit to England. 'I have never feared anything more than I did my return to Ireland a week later. I was convinced, as I had never been in France, that I was going to be killed and, which was worse, that I should be killed without a chance to defend myself. I longed passionately for some way of escape, but there was obviously none and I cursed the Irish Channel in a misery of nervous tension.' This may

47

simply have been the result of six years of stress; alternatively, it may be that the courage which enables a man to lead his troops on the Western Front in an attack at dawn is quite different from that which is needed to deal with 'the smiler with the knife'.

The latter was probably true of Pope, for when he got back to Dublin he discovered that an independent Company was to be formed out of the detachments of tanks and armoured cars scattered over the south of Ireland, and that he was to command it with his headquarters in Cork. The point is that Pope welcomed the change, in spite of the fact that Cork had a far worse reputation for violence than Dublin. But he would have an active command, personal responsibility and the means for hitting back. The future Field-Marshal Montgomery became Brigade Major of the Cork Infantry Brigade about that time, and in his biography of Montgomery Alan Moorehead has well summarized the conditions in the south: 'It was impossible to carry out normal military tactics since the Sinn Feiners wore civilian clothes, and having carried out an ambush simply vanished among the ordinary crowds of the city. They made night attacks on isolated British outposts, kidnapped policemen, destroyed bridges, dug trenches across roads and threw bombs into military buildings. Week by week the hatred on all sides grew more bitter.' By comparison with the indiscriminate murder campaign in Ulster fifty years later such events seem small in scope, but it was Britain's first experience of a modern guerrilla. By the 1960s the army had much practical experience of such matters and was psychologically prepared. For Pope and his fellows the experience was novel, and the more taxing precisely because of its novelty.

Nor, indeed, as Moorehead's description suggests, was the situation in the south any improvement on that in and around Dublin. But during the next eighteen months Pope was never brought so near to the breaking-point again. His headquarters were in Cork, where he had under command some ten officers and 120 men, with a miscellaneous collection of tanks and armoured cars. But what probably kept him sane was the fact that the total area for which he was responsible ranged from Waterford to Galway. Thus he had many scattered detachments to visit, and though such trips were often dangerous he was able to move about constantly and to avoid the claustrophobia of continual life in a city, with gunmen potentially lurking everywhere to assassinate a marked man like himself.

This is not to say that the strain, as it turned out, was any less than it had been further north. Indeed Pope admitted that his nerves were continuously on edge; the assassin was always there in the shadows, and after a County Inspector had been shot down in the Cork Club no haven seemed secure. He lived in a block of houses in Cork occupied by members of the Military Courts, a nest of judges and prosecutors which seemed a sitting target for a Sinn Fein bomb. Nevertheless, up to and after the signing of the Treaty in December, 1921, (since the IRA prolonged its militant campaign for a Republic long after the Irish Free State emerged) Pope was able to keep going largely because his command allowed him to be active. There was always an outpost to visit, a raid to organize, a suspect to run to ground.

One Sunday morning that summer two constables of the RIC were murdered in cold blood, by the usual gentlemen in trench-coats, as they took their glass in the local bar. One staggered into the street and lay there dying. A passing priest who gave him comfort was threatened by the killers, but stayed to the end. Pope immediately organized a raiding party, which by quick action corralled a couple of dozen suspicious characters. 'I lined the men up in the street and told them of the murder committed that day. "You will," I said, "I am sure, agree that now is an admirable time for avenging that murder, and if we were to adopt your tactics I should ask you to select four or five of your number to be shot against that wall. That is the kind of war you appreciate and, by God, I really don't know why you shouldn't have a taste of your own medicine. Luckily for you, however, we are soldiers who have an absurd prejudice against shooting unresisting men in the back and who regard murder as cowardly."' Instead, after thorough cross-questioning, he took back to Cork a few of the most obvious ring-leaders.

Pope must certainly have used more crisp and soldierly language in his little address than he recorded in his memoirs, but the episode serves well to illustrate the dilemma which faces all officers of humane instincts who are involved in 'peace-keeping' activities, whether it be Cork and Dublin in 1921, or Palestine in the 'thirties, or Cyprus, or Ulster after 1969. Pope was not a ruthless mercenary, he was the complete, professional soldier, with the loyalties and sense of duty of his caste, but he was also a man, liberal-minded, speculative, sensitive. He deeply loathed the excesses of the Black and Tans and the Auxiliaries, and despised even more the double-talk of politicians in Parliament who concealed those excesses with words. On the other hand he was outraged by the work of the Sinn Fein and the IRA, whose bloody evidence was so often before his eyes. Since rebellion must be put down, his own preference was for firm, legitimate but decisive action, and no fumbling; the initiative must be grasped and never lost. 'Instead', he noted, 'of crushing Sinn Fein by a few blows delivered by resolution we were hardening the people, accustoming them to violence, and following vaguely in the wake of terrorism. We were always too late in our restrictive measures.' Even more did he feel a sense of frustration when, after the signing of the Treaty, the murder of British sympathizers, police, and even British soldiers continued while the British Army was virtually powerless to hit back. It is significant that of this time he wrote, 'I was sick at heart', and that in a letter to his father from Cork on 3 March, 1922, the future Field-Marshal Montgomery declared, 'It really is most degrading for us soldiers having to stay on here.'

Relief came at last. He was asked by the War Office if he was prepared to go out to Egypt to take command of the 3rd Armoured Car Company. 'At last I was free and I went from Cork to Dublin and from Dublin to the packet-boat with eager delight. Folly and cruelty, bitterness and hatred, I had suffered these to the full in Russia and Ireland, but tomorrow is a new day and I was leaving them behind me at last. I forgot that yesterday was a new day, once, and that men remain men.'

CHAPTER FIVE

CAIRO TO CAMBERLEY

The armoured car was the convenient chariot of war for the immediate post-war period. Tanks were unsuited to the times. Britain's main military tasks overseas were policing and peace-keeping, for which the mastodons of Cambrai and August, 1918, even in the best and latest Mark V version, were too cumbrous, too slow and too expensive. The financial stringency of the 'twenties, moreover, combined with War Office conservatism to prevent the development of smaller and faster models to the point at which quantity production might have cut down cost. There was a gap in military ecology which the armoured car comfortably fitted.

It was no newcomer to the environment. Since the Royal Naval Air Service in 1914 manoeuvred steel-plated improvisations along the Belgian coast, many thousands of armoured cars had been constructed before 1918 by most of the combatant nations and many future functions were explored. (After 1917 the Russians even had a half-tracked type, which was used in the Russo-Polish war of 1920.) There was, for example, the Duke of Westminster's dramatic 120-mile dash with his Rolls Royces across the North African desert to rescue prisoners held by the Senussi at Bir Hacheim. There was T. E. Lawrence's creative use of his hard-worked cars along the road to Damascus. And, from the point of view of the 'armoured idea', perhaps the most striking instance was the saving from murder by his Tartar captors in March, 1918 of a Major P. C. S. Hobart; the plane in which 'Hobo' was a passenger had been shot down from behind the Turkish lines in Mesopotamia, and his life was preserved only at the last minute by the chance appearance of an armoured car patrol which had been sent out to operate on a 100-mile range in search of him. Looking over the next quarter of a century, it is impossible to conceive how British armour might have developed without Hobart's many-sided genius.

In every sense, therefore, Pope's posting to the 3rd Armoured Car Company in Egypt was opportune—and symbolic—because just as he was to advance, over the next two decades, to a high personal position in the armoured command, so his Company would grow into the 6th Battalion, Royal Tank Regiment, and become an original member of the Desert Rats of 7th Armoured Division. The posting was opportune psychologically, because he had known no peace since 1914, and he was jaded and strained. But, since Britain herself was theoretically at peace, a torpid home station was not the best place in which to begin to assimilate his new career. In Egypt, by contrast, there was space to train realistically, relative freedom from Whitehall, and a world for exploration far different from Passchendaele, Tundra or Cork. Moreover, there was a sense of being involved in something real, for armoured cars were now employed far and wide—on the North-West Frontier, for example. In Iraq Trenchard's passionate claim that the RAF could keep the peace more economically than the Army had been tested and proved; as part of that successful effort armoured cars of the RAF's own manufacture were in regular use. And only recently, in the summer of 1921, the 4th AC Company from Palestine (sister to the 3rd) had helped the RAF to mark a route across the Syrian Desert as far as Baghdad.

When Pope arrived at Abbassia Barracks in Cairo in March, 1922, he had a stroke of luck. His Adjutant—for in those days an Armoured Car Company possessed such luxuries—was a Captain Briggs. The future Major-General Raymond Briggs, CB, DSO, would spend the next quarter of a century, like Pope, in distinguished service as a man of armour, and unlike Pope would have the good fortune to win a reputation in action with the Eighth Army, particularly by his handling of 1st Armoured Division at Alamein and the Mareth Line. Like Pope he had also served throughout the First War, in the infantry and the Machine Gun Corps, transferring to the Tank Corps in 1920. Their paths would cross at important points in 1940 and 1941. Pope was thus very lucky to find at his side, when he took over his first substantial armoured command, a man of Briggs' qualities who had a natural affinity for 'the armoured idea'.

Briggs, for his part, was at first not so sure about his own luck. Who could this one-armed manifestation be, arriving to run a mobile unit? The DSO and the MC on Pope's tunic told their story, of course; one might be a mistake, but hardly two. As for the missing arm, Briggs recalled other officers who had been kept on with similar disqualifications. But the contrast with his previous (and more lackadaisical) Colonel soon became evident, as Pope's sensible but searching efficiency revealed itself and the temper of his mind became plain. Already, however, that reserve which he was to carry like a garment had begun to enfold him, for the initial impression he made on Briggs was of a contained personality whose defences were not easily penetrated.

On the other hand his Company was certainly not confined. On the contrary, during the following months Pope was writing meticulous reports on patrols and reconnaissances well into the desert surrounding Cairo, and eastwards into Sinai. To read such reports is a vivid reminder of the immense advantage which the British ought to have held over the Germans in North Africa from 1941 onwards. Until the *Afrika Korps* disembarked at Tripoli none of its members—certainly no officer of significance, and certainly no unit—knew anything at all about the desert. Not merely were they ignorant of the modes of warfare in this special and demanding terrain; they approached as virgins the simplest problems of desert housewifery. They had no practice in navigation. They could only guess at what was involved in maintaining guns and tanks and transport in this novel world of heat and dust. But the British had a constantly renewed tradition of presence and practice in the desert dating from pre-1918. Pope's tentative sorties in 1922 were only the forerunners of many such, so that by 1940, when the Western Desert Force first faced its Italian enemies, the British Army was not unprovided with leaders for whom the desert was a natural home. It was unfortunate that so valuable an advantage was sometimes thrown away, and that the basic professional skills and attitudes of the Germans enabled them to adapt swiftly and almost instinctively to this strange theatre, just as they came to terms with the winter hell of Russia.

Unlike the Germans in 1941, Pope and his men in 1922 at least had the opportunity of beginning in the Kindergarten and learning gradually in peace instead of hurriedly in war. 'The main object of the patrol,' he wrote in a report in June, 'was to exercise all ranks in desert patrolling; the use of the aeroplane compass, construction of bivouacs, desert driving, passage of natural obstacles etc, etc.' The detailed notes which follow on petrol and water consumption, tyre endurance and so on have an elementary character until one realizes how little information about these matters was then available in the British or any other army. And, simple as they may sound, the following 'lessons learned' have a permanent truth which any Desert Rat of the Second World War would immediately recognize:

'(1) No difficult country should ever be attempted if any practicable way round exists. It is quicker and less arduous to make a wide detour than to push, pull and drag an armoured car out of soft sand. All dubious places must therefore be reconnoitred on foot, the car remaining on firm ground until it is decided whether a crossing is feasible at that point.

(2) Time and energy will be saved by crossing *wadis* at their heads and highest points rather than attempting them lower down.

(3) Shingly desert when the stones are freely but not closely scattered is treacherous and should be avoided.

(4) If bad ground must be crossed it is quicker and less tiring to lay down wire tracks over the worst patches before attempting to cross them.

(5) If it is necessary to cross dubious ground without laying down any tracks or other form of resistance, the car must be lightened of all unnecessary loads, driven at the obstacle whole-heartedly and kept moving. Half-hearted methods invariably lead to disaster.'

Pope put his finger on another basic truth about desert navigation when later in the year he wrote after another patrol: 'I would again emphasize the fact that the only certain method of traversing the Western Desert is by compass and speedometer. Alleged "landmarks" may be classed with old car tracks rather as dangers than aids to navigation. The desert seen at dawn is misleadingly different from the same view at dusk and movement through ten degrees of a compass will change a conical into a flat topped hill and a prominent bluff into a vaguely undulating

1. Vyvyan Pope as a subaltern in full dress uniform, after he had been commissioned into the North Staffordshire Regiment.

2. A vehicle of the 3rd Armoured Company in 1922.

3. A 3rd Armoured Company Rolls Royce Armoured Car.

plateau.' None of the sophistication of the Long Range Desert Group, acquired twenty years later during their phenomenal journeys, would have led them to challenge these fundamental facts.

Another foretaste of future operations occurred in October. During the 'sixties and 'seventies that area of northern Sinai from El Arish to the Mitla Pass was of intense concern to the Israelis in their conflicts with Egypt, and it was here that forty years earlier Pope carried out a careful reconnaissance in light cars which resulted in a minute report on the terrain and its feasibility for military operations. The importance of these relatively small-scale ventures was twofold—though their scale is less reduced if it be compared with what was militarily normal in 1922. First, it meant that Pope's mind was able to shake free from the limited horizons imposed on an infantryman by the Western Front, where an advance of a hundred yards was an achievement and a thousand yards was stupendous. Secondly, he was being imperceptibly prepared for the doctrines which men like Fuller and Liddell Hart were already developing in England, of free-ranging mobile forces possessing a strategic potentiality in their own right. It was, it may be recalled, from a similar intense study of motorization and the implications of mobility that Guderian moved on to his own concept of armoured formations. Nor is it surprising that while Pope was feeling his way in Egypt George Lindsay, whom Liddell Hart was to describe as 'one of the foremost advocates of armoured warfare', was already carrying out in Iraq, as commander of No. 1 Armoured Car Group, experiments in using a mechanized force combined with aircraft and entirely maintained by air supply.

It was a good thing Pope had this opportunity to shake loose in Egypt, for in December he returned to England and, so far as armour was concerned, to a far more stagnant situation. The following year, 1923, was one of consolidation, of establishing more firmly a jumping-off point into the future, rather than one of experiment and advance. Until now, indeed, armour's foundations had been shaky, since unlike the other arms, infantry, cavalry and artillery, tanks had so far had no definite status. It was not until 1 September, 1923, that the Tank Corps was constituted on an official and permanent footing, signalized two months later by the grant from the King of the prefix 'Royal', and the adoption as a distinctive headdress of the black beret. Much of this period, therefore, was taken up by reorganization, selection of new officers for the Corps, establishment of permanent headquarters and the other housekeeping arrangements which attended official recognition.

Not that this recognition was generous. Only four battalions were allocated to the Corps, the 2nd (at Farnborough), 3rd (at Lydd), 4th (at Wareham), and 5th (at Tidworth). The 1st became a 'Depot' and had to wait a decade before resuscitation. It was to the 4th Battalion at Wareham that Pope was posted. He was temporarily in the doldrums. To begin with, the yeast of the new doctrines about mobile warfare had as yet hardly begun to ferment, and as yet Pope was not known and accepted by the inner circle of pioneers. There was nothing intellectually or militarily stimulating in which to get involved. And secondly, the general run of officers in the Tank Corps was at this time unsatisfactory. The reason, of course, was that the wartime Corps had been largely filled by officers on temporary commissions, the greater part of whom naturally departed back to civilian life. With few regular officers remaining, a call had to be put out by the War Office in the spring of 1923 for officers who wished to transfer, and it was not, in fact, until the Tank Corps became a permanent entity in September that the last gazetting to complete its establishment was carried out. Many of the incomers were inadequate.

'Besides officers already serving with the Corps, it attracted a number of first-rate officers from other arms who were keen about the tank idea. But it also attracted a rather large number of officers who had applied for transfer merely because they could see little or no chance of being promoted in their own corps or regiments. Unfortunately, the enthusiasts tended to be in the junior grades, while too many of the others got into the upper grade by virtue merely of their length of military service. That top-hamper became a serious handicap on the Corps in the years that followed. A very high proportion of majors had to be passed over as not qualified to command. Such slow-minded soldiers, thinking more of their pastimes and pensions than of progress, were a hindrance in the development of fast-moving tactics.'*

Pope was living, in fact, in an Army lacerated and lopped by the Geddes Axe. As infantry regiments, for example, concertina'd in size from four to two battalions there was inevitably an excess of officers, and it was inevitably those least certain of, and usually least qualified for, promotion in their own units who sought a brighter future for themselves in the Royal Tank Corps. Remembering Pope's scathing comments on the type of officer with whom he had to mix when he first came to Wareham in 1920 to work with armoured cars one is not surprised that 1923 was also a phase lacking in amenity.

The troops with whom he had to deal were, by and large, of a different calibre. Major-General Horace Birks was an instructor at the RTC Centre at Bovington in 1923—it was here that he first met Pope, when the latter arrived on a

* Liddell Hart, *The Tanks*, Vol. I, p. 225.

course—and he recalls this difference in quality. A main reason was the fact of economic depression. Recruits were not scarce, and for mechanically-minded men of good type from Birmingham and other industrial areas the Tank Corps had a special pull. Pope was not handling trash, an impression one might gain from reading T. E. Lawrence's letters. Lawrence was at Bovington in 1923, under his cover-name of T. E. Shaw. Birks remembers him well: 'a short man, red-faced, in the Quartermaster's stores'. But Lawrence's letters seem to be written more out of self-hate than objective scrutiny:

'Here every man has joined because he was down and out: and no one talks of the Army or of promotion, or of trades and accomplishments. We are all here unavoidably, in a last resort, and we assume this world's failure in one another, so that pretence would be not merely laughed at, but as near an impossibility as anything human. We are social bed-rock, those unfit for life-by-competition: and each of us values the rest as cheap as he knows himself to be.'*

Was Lawrence in the ranks of the Tank Corps *unavoidably*?

It will be remembered that when he was in Ireland Pope had opted for the Tank Corps primarily because this seemed to offer the best avenue to the Staff College. The option succeeded, for in January, 1924, he obtained a place on the Camberley course. To a future commander the value of his time at the College may perhaps be assessed partly by the quality of his own performance, and partly by the quality of his contemporaries—and by their assessment of him. Pope's performance was outstanding. He and a future VCIGS, (then Captain A. E. Nye, MC, of the Royal Warwickshire Regiment), came out top of the

* Letter to Lionel Curtis, 27 March, 1923.

list, and it was Nye who was to say to his son many years later that 'of your father's generation he was the one who was going to become CIGS.' As to contemporaries, it was, to begin with, no small thing to have, as Commandant, Ironside, young for the job and still fresh from his unorthodox eastern adventures, or to have, as instructor, 'Boney' Fuller, whose selection in 1925 by the new CIGS, Field-Marshal Sir George Milne, as his Military Assistant 'was taken by the Army in general as a signal of his intention to carry out the mechanization of the Army, with the tank in the principal role. It startled many of his contemporaries who had persistently denounced the new gospel as heresy.'[*] Milne never, of course, fulfilled those expectations. All the same, for Pope in 1924 and 1925, Fuller at Camberley was the right man in the right place.

But Ironside and Fuller were of the directorate—as were Alan Brooke, Lindsell and Ronald Adam. Among his fellow students, however, one also finds many names of future distinction, men like Messervy, Godwin-Austen, Otto Lund, O'Moore Creagh, Scobie, Noel Irwin, Beresford-Peirse and Tuker. Since the Staff College, like a university, achieves its results partly through the education of its students by its students, Pope was fortunate to find himself amid such stimulating and capable company. Moreover, his success in surpassing them made him thereafter a marked man. There is one name, incidentally, which stands out in the list. For the 1924–25 season of the Staff College Drag Hunt the Master was a Major C. W. M. Norrie of the 11th Hussars (later to become Lieut-General the Lord Norrie GCMG, GCVO, CB, DSO, MC).[†] After Pope's death in 1941 it was, of course, General

---

[*] Liddell Hart, *Memoirs*, Vol. 1, p. 99.
[†] 'Comparisons are odious but I always thought he was one of the bright boys and he and Archie Nye were about the two best.' Lord Norrie, letter to the author, 15.1.74.

Norrie who hastily took over his armoured corps to fight the CRUSADER battle.

Mention of the 'Drag' is a reminder of the excessive and, in retrospect, absurd prestige attached at the Staff College of those day to prowess in the hunting field—a reflection of the disastrous dominance of the British Army between the wars by a cavalry which was already out of date in 1914. Pope's lack of an arm at least saved him from becoming one who, as Shakespeare put it in *The Merchant of Venice*, 'doth nothing but talk of his horse'. Since sport was out of the question, he could neither be tempted to partake nor criticized for abstaining; nor, which is much more to the point, could he be seduced by 'the cavalry spirit' into such an abrogation of professional judgement as Haig committed with his notorious confession: 'I am all for using aeroplanes and tanks, but they are only accessories to the man and the horse, and I feel sure that as time goes on you will find just as much use for the horse—the well-bred horse—as you have ever done in the past'.

Instead, he worked—and played in his own way. The wry sense of humour which had sustained him in the trenches was still alive, and would remain so to the end. (It was in the late 'thirties that he observed to the historian Sir Charles Petrie how fatal it was to let enthusiasts about armour *talk* to people. Fuller, Hobart and Martel, he argued, should be locked in an upper room at the War Office, and fed from time to time with written questions to which they would reply with written answers which would probably be correct. But, he said, they must never be allowed to *talk*.) One outlet he now found in *Owl Pie*, the annual journal written by members of the Staff College for other members and their predecessors. Pope's own copy of the number for Christmas, 1925, is of some interest, because although contributions were anonymous he pencilled in the names of most of the authors. Thus we find a letter addressed from 'HMS *Queen Elizabeth*, Mediterranean Fleet', which must be one of the earlier published works by Stephen King Hall. Several lively pieces turn out to be by Godwin-Austen, a foretaste of the famous birthday message which, as a Lieutenant-General, he despatched to Winston Churchill in November, 1941, when CRUSADER reached its climax: 'Corridor to Tobruk clear and secure. Tobruk is as relieved as I am'. Pope himself contributed a Shakespearean skit, and also 'Don Juan At The Staff College: a Byronic Fragment', which after examining Juan's vicissitudes as a student ended neatly:

'O Personality, what dreary crimes
  Are solemnly committed in thy name!
Old men in Clubs write letters to *The Times*;
  And young ones prose and pose and deal out blame;
Or—what's still worse—they take to scribbling rhymes;
  And all to win a casual glance from Fame!
Each to his choice! Juan achieved renown
By drinking whiskey, standing upside-down.

But what befell thereafter—how he fought
  More battles than Napoleon ever knew,
And very seldom did as he was taught
  And yet escaped a well-earned Waterloo,
Until at last (after a deal of thought)
  He was enrolled among the Chosen Few
Who carry, let us hope, in their portmanteau
A Marshal's baton—That's another canto.'

There was, as it happened, another Pope on the same course, though no relation: Captain and Brevet Major Maurice Pope, MC, of the Royal Canadian Engineers, who was later to become a Lieutenant-General and, after a notable military career, to serve as Canadian Ambassador to Belgium and then to Spain. The namesakes became firm and lasting friends. While at the Staff College they made two continental journeys together, which revealed to the Canadian interesting facets of a character which he too had found cloaked by reserve, putting this down to the effect of losing a right arm.

To begin with, Maurice Pope experienced over many European miles the true significance of Vyvyan's passion, in spite of his single arm, for driving a car at high speed —a passion which sometimes made lesser men, after a typical run, demand a stiff whisky before they were prepared to alight. 'He knew the rules of the road and observed them, but no road hog ever successfully crowded him. He once said that he had a good sense of time and space and could confidently drive to within one inch of an oncoming car without the slightest danger to himself. Consequently, when meeting one that was selfishly taking more than its fair share of the road V.V. would drive straight at him, confident that his skill would enable him to swerve in time ... He was never proved wrong ... He often lit a cigarette, unaided, when rolling along at a speed of fifty miles an hour, and more.'

Their first trip took them from Antwerp down to Nice, and from there to the tables of Monte Carlo, where Maurice played with modest stakes for a modest gain. But when he sought out Vyvyan, 'With a flushed face he was waving 1000 franc notes on to the table from a large pile he had before him. An onlooker remarked that but a few moments previously his winnings were twice as great as they were now.' Yet this was the man who also confessed to his Canadian friend that he had been most unhappy during his first term at Camberley, finding the close scrutiny of the directing staff irksome because he felt he was being judged not only by the quality of the work he submitted but also by his speech, manners, appearance and general bearing. Pope was, in fact, a cavalier, but a complicated and hypersensitive specimen of the breed.

For their second trip, in August, 1925, they were joined by Archie Nye, and motored from Antwerp to Budapest, Vyvyan's avowed purpose being 'to gain a better knowledge of the geography of Middle and Eastern Europe'. Somewhere east of Prague they put up for the night at an inn in a small garrison town, and retired late after sitting up drinking with the commanding officer of the local cavalry regiment. 'When Nye and I came down to breakfast the following morning,' Maurice Pope recalled, 'we were met by a dishevelled, bleary-eyed and ferocious V. V. Pope. He had been up all night, he griped, fighting bed-bugs! They were so bad, he said, that he had had to spend most of the night sitting on an un-upholstered chair in the middle of the room. He even brought us up to his room to show us five specimens he had caged inside an upturned glass.' As the others showed little sympathy, Pope insisted on their spending the next night in the most palatial hotel in Budapest. This they did, after a nightmare race with a Hungarian car during which Pope took at least one corner on two wheels.

At home he would sometimes shed his inhibitions in a similar fashion. Major-General Lionel Finch was also a contemporary at the Staff College. They were not particularly close. 'Being a bit reserved myself, I expect it was natural that I sensed reserve in him, and made no attempt to penetrate it. There is, however, one episode that remains in my memory. One day we were all out in the country together, somewhere near Newbury, engaged in some tactical exercise. Having a few hours to spare, Pope took me and a couple of others in his powerful car up onto the top of the Berkshire Downs. There he gave us a wonderful display of skilful and daring driving—frightening us not a little. I remember watching the speedometer hover around 70 mph (a pretty good speed for those days) as we skirted rabbit holes, jumped over shallow ditches, etc. Nothing very remarkable about that, you may say. But the fact was that he was steering with his chest pressed against the wheel, his single arm being busy with the gears, brakes, etc. I suppose one could draw conclusions from this display as to his personal character. One would be that under his quiet exterior there was a man who enjoyed taking risks, not only for himself but for other people!'*

The value of these recollections is that they bring out in a fresh way that devil-may-care quality in Pope which comes out so vividly in his own memoir of '14–'18. It was a quality held in balance by his intellect, his aesthetic interests and his straightforward professionalism as a soldier, but it was there to be tapped. The intellect and the professionalism had made their point, for in spite of the intense scrutiny to which he had been subjected by the directing staff at Camberley he emerged, as has been seen, with flying colours. It was a result of his success that in April, 1926, he found himself appointed to a key post, that of Brigade Major to the Royal Tank Corps Centre at Bovington.

He took with him a bride, whom he had wooed in a manner so subtle (as he thought) but so completely transparent that her family must already have decided that he was a satisfactory suitor. While he was at the Staff College he met Sybil Moore, the niece of acquaintances of his mother. She was 14 years younger than himself—still, in fact, studying singing at the Guildhall School of Music in London. How could he get time with her on his own, in a seemly fashion? He announced to her relatives that the moment had come for her to learn to drive, and he would teach her. The implausible idea of a one-armed man

* Letter to the author.

teaching one's young niece to drive—in the ponderous machines of 1925—worked so well that they were married early in 1926 and went straight from honeymoon to Bovington.

In fact the lessons were less absurd than might appear, for Sybil Pope found her husband to be an instinctive and immaculate driver. During the many thousands of miles they travelled together in his cars she never had a second's anxiety. Indeed, the absence of a right arm was neither an impediment nor a frustration. He could do everything for which two hands are normally required, grease his own car, tie his own evening ties, except one—he was unable to replace an electric light bulb. To his wife it seemed an entirely natural situation when, one year, it was only the fact of other commitments which prevented him, as he had intended, from taking part in the Monte Carlo Rally!

CHAPTER SIX

THE GREEN FIELDS BEYOND*

Major-General Nigel Duncan should be a good judge of a man of armour, having himself transferred from the Black Watch to the Royal Tank Corps in 1923, served with distinction as one of its most forward-looking officers, and become Director of the Royal Armoured Corps and Colonel-Commandant of the Royal Tank Regiment. In 1926, as a Lieutenant, he was Adjutant of the Royal Tank Corps Centre at Bovington when Vyvyan Pope arrived as Brigade Major, and it was in the nature of their work that the young officer should have observed at close quarters this be-ribboned, armless veteran whose reputation for personal bravery and professional ability had preceded him. Duncan was not disillusioned.

'He was so clearly a master of all that he did. There was a finish to all his work, a feeling such as one gets in the presence of a great craftsman. It all seemed so simple when he expounded his views. I was a Staff College Candidate at the time and I used to go to him for instruction in the evenings, and this was quite fascinating. He was so direct and clear in his explanations that those of us who attended his classes became

---

* General Elles designed Colours for the Tank Corps and flew them on his tank when he personally led the Corps into action at Cambrai. The brown, red and green were subsequently alleged by Fuller to represent 'From mud, through blood, to the green fields beyond.'

quite absorbed. Mobility and speed were his great watchwords. I suppose that his experiences in France had influenced him but he was always much in favour of movement, almost at any price, with the concomitant need for officers to have speed in thought both in decision and action. All this sounds very trite now, but in those days of slow deliberate attack, and ponderous orders which made obeisance to Staff Duties, it was almost revolutionary. Gradually I got to know him better and he talked more freely on armoured warfare, where he was an advanced thinker for the times.*

For a man with such an approach, Pope had come to the Tank Centre at exactly the right moment. During the two years he was at Bovington the force of the more enlightened post-war thinking about armour at last began to make some impression on the military Establishment. The early practitioners of 1917–1918, and the later theorists, Fuller, Martel, Broad, Liddell Hart, Lindsay now saw the start, if only on a minor scale, of a fulfilment of their dreams. To be revolutionary was still to be considered odd, but it no longer necessarily involved being ruled out of court. Two years earlier and Pope would have found the climate of opinion less propitious.

The warmth of the new climate was at first deceptively favourable, for Milne's early utterances and attitudes when he became CIGS, and his choice of Fuller as Assistant, seemed to promise a strong drive from the top in the direction of mechanization and mobility. Though Milne soon chose a seat on the fence, the after-effects remained, for, as the Russians later found in Hungary and Czechoslovakia, once the spirit of liberalism is allowed to run free it is extraordinarily difficult to bottle it up again. In the Secretary of State's speech on the Army Estimates in

* Letter to the author.

March, 1926, he therefore announced that an experimental armoured force was to be formed; and though dilatoriness and doubt delayed the formation for another year, though the arrangements for its command were botched, and though it only carried out exercises for a meagre few weeks, nevertheless the Experimental Mechanized Force which came together on Salisbury Plain in the summer of 1928 was, as Liddell Hart puts it in *The Tanks*, 'The first mechanized formation to be born in the world and . . . the mother of all "armoured divisions".' Of all these developments Pope, from his pivotal position at the Royal Tank Corps Centre, was an intimate eye-witness. To have been able to watch the formation and training of this pioneer group was of special significance to him in that when he, in his turn, came to command the Mobile Force assembled at Mersa Matruh in 1936, as a result of the Abyssinian crisis, he would in fact be at the head of the first such force ever mobilized by Great Britain for what might prove to be war. Thus these two years were of seminal importance.

The misfortune of being a forward thinker is that with the benefit of hindsight all his perceptions can be made to appear painfully obvious. But in the mid-twenties little in the field of modern armoured theory and practice was obvious—except to a few. It required some imagination, for example, to believe in the possibility of *speed* and *range* for tanks. So far there had been few actual demonstrations,* for the slow-moving monsters of the Western Front were no evidence and the great armoured assault planned by Fuller for 1919 never took place. But Pope had grasped this basic theme of the new doctrines, and he was also emphatic about specific deficiencies, some of which would take years to make good. For example, he

* The Medium C and D tanks had demonstrated the possibilities, and the Vickers Medium, now well into production, revealed the potentialities.

saw clearly that the exercises of the Experimental Force had exposed a need for infantry carried in tracked and armoured vehicles to take advantage of the openings made by tanks. This concept, now made conventional in most armies by the possibility of nuclear war, was not put into practical effect by the British until 1944—preceded, inevitably, by the Germans. Pope was at one with Liddell Hart, with Pile and the rest of the small group who in 1927 argued the case for armoured infantry, but their ideas were discarded and deferred, to be overtaken in the 'thirties by the move to motorize the British infantry. Until 1944, therefore, the armoured divisions went into action supported by infantry in trucks, or, at best, the vulnerable Bren-gun carrier.

Then there was the question of artillery support for armour. The Germans appreciated this requirement and, at the simplest level, provided their armoured divisions with tanks (i.e. guns on tracks) which could fire high explosive as well as solid shot. Even at this simplest level, it was not until the Americans provided Grants and Shermans in 1942 that the British possessed in quantity a tank whose gun could fire the invaluable high explosive shell, nor was it until the Americans again provided equipment that the British had the use of a self-propelled gun. Throughout the 'twenties and 'thirties, in fact, the British military establishment relied on the ordinary unprotected field-gun as a support for tanks. In consequence, as many gunners found to their cost in North Africa, the naked 25-pounder had to be employed in armoured battles, towed into action by an unarmoured vehicle with the gun pointing in the wrong direction.

Yet there was a solution, revealed as early as 1925 in that year's Army Manoeuvres. This was the Birch gun, which took its name from the horse-artilleryman who at that time was Master-General of the Ordnance, Sir Noel

Birch. The 'Birch' was an 18-pounder field-gun mounted on a turntable within the chassis of a Vickers Medium tank, and in later versions the gun-crew was fully protected by armour.* This weapon had several capabilities—as a normal field-gun, as an anti-tank gun, as a 'close assault' gun, even as an anti-aircraft gun. If the promise of its trials was not fully realized in its performance, nevertheless there was no inherent flaw in the basic idea, as the Germans and Americans were to prove. The 'Birch' could have been developed into a viable weapon. Unfortunately the current jealousies between the artillery and the armoured idealists caused the enterprise to be still-born, thus, in the British way, leaving the army inadequately equipped and providing the opportunity for gallant men to win the Victoria Cross at the cost of their lives.

We see now that this was a critical error. But Pope *at the time* was quite clear, as General Duncan witnesses, about the importance of the Birch gun. 'It was a lasting worry to him that the Royal Artillery missed their opportunity over this weapon which would have made such a difference.' So, in 1940, he would see the urgent need for up-gunning British armour with the 6-pounder gun though even this lacked the versatility of the Birch gun. And he was strongly advocating at this time the need for a system of control which allowed, as Duncan puts it, 'the general use of wireless telephones for officer-to-officer conversations on commander level'. Here he was with Hobart, who wrote to Lindsay on 10 July, 1925: 'Until we have means of commanding and controlling tanks on the move, we cannot be a formation or force, but only an unco-ordinated crowd of units in action. However good individuals are, this is as unsatisfactory as Naval measures before Kempenfeld's time.' Such methods of control and command are,

* For the design see Kenneth Macksey and John H. Batchelor, *Tank: a History of the Armoured Fighting Vehicle*, (Macdonald, 1970) p. 95.

of course, a modern commonplace, but how far ahead Pope was in his thinking may be illustrated by the fact that it was not until the Tank Brigade manoeuvres of the 'thirties that the methods were experimentally proved—with an inadequate number of inefficient sets, and with communication from tank to tank occasionally being effected by a child's fishing net on the end of a long stick.

'All this', as Nigel Duncan writes, 'sounds very trite now.' The imagination has to be stretched hard to envisage a time when you were something of a prophet, and often suspect at that, if you advocated not only the need but the actual possibility of fast-moving tanks manoeuvring in large controlled bodies, directed by a single commander with officer-to-officer wireless communication, and supported by self-propelled guns and protected infantry capable of keeping pace with, and alive amid, an armoured battle. Yet Pope was preaching no more than these well-established commonplaces of the mid-century. He was an instance of the rare but invaluable soldier who can shed the preconceptions of his training and experience and grasp, at an early stage, the basic principles of a new pattern of war. For most of his contemporaries the jump from the mentality of the trenches to an understanding of armoured mobility was difficult to make. Indeed, there were generals, both German and British, who had not made it by 1939.

There was another reason why 1926 was a good year for Pope to take up his new post. The Royal Tank Corps was beginning to find itself. After three years of formal existence it was starting to see itself not as an oddity but as an entity. 'We had had long enough', Duncan recalled, 'to stop saying "We don't do things like that in *my* regiment" and to begin to think which way we would do things in *our* Corps. It was all fertile ground for V.V. . . . Indeed as we became a little more influential everyone loved us less until it became borne in on us that if we had to survive we had to be so good, so much masters of our job that we couldn't be done away with. The realization of this, with the new drive for better efficiency in which V.V. was of course a leading exponent, set the whole place alight.'

There was an energetic new Brigadier in charge of the Centre, Kenneth Laird, new Commanding officers at the Depot and the various schools, and a new training programme.

This upsurge of self-confidence was, indeed, also finding its reflection in the new quality of officer. The day was still to come when the Tank Corps would actually be able to select its officers from an excess of admirable applicants, but the shift in this direction was already visible. The interim period of the early 'twenties which had caused Pope so much professional distaste, the time when the Tank Corps was in danger of becoming a dump for undesirables, the implicit sense of inferiority—all these were now in process of fading away. Years had still to pass, but the green fields smiled beyond. At Alamein half the British armour consisted of Royal Tank Regiments (ten complete and three sub-units), while two of the three armoured divisional commanders (Briggs and Gatehouse) and four of the armoured brigade commanders, (Custance, Kenchington, Richards and Roberts) came from the RTR. Moreover, the new stress on efficiency and *esprit de corps* which was initiated by Pope and his colleagues in the latter 'twenties, and given new impetus by Hobart in the 'thirties, meant that many of the other armoured units in the Second World War—the cavalry, the Yeomanry— owed much of their skills to the Tank Corps men who had been seconded to them or had supervised their training.

Licking into shape an embryonic organization demands special qualities in the organizer of which ruthlessness, impatience and perfectionism are inevitable elements. Hobart could be terrible in his wrath. Wingate, creating his Chindits against the clock, could be unforgivable in his urgency. Pope, in spite of those deep human sympathies which this memoir had already disclosed, was too professional a soldier to suffer fools gladly or to gloss over incompetence. His time at the Centre was a time for getting things right in the Tank Corps. This came first. 'He had a trick', Nigel Duncan noted, 'which fascinated me, of listening to news which displeased him with a frown that grew fiercer and fiercer with the intensity of his gaze. When you finished he pursed up his lips and made a funny pop-ish sound. Something between Poo and Bla. It indicated extreme displeasure and was followed by an outburst of wrath directed at the source of displeasure. I took very good care that no sin of either omission or commission of mine was the cause. The outburst over, it was succeded by either a vitriolic letter or visit, the facts having been noted in his awful hand in a little black loose-leaf notebook which he continually annotated or emended.'*

After this spasm of intense and satisfying activity Pope was transferred to what, by comparison, was a stagnant pool. In June, 1928, he joined the staff of Southern Command as GSO 2. There could be nothing dynamic in a formation whose GOC was Montgomery-Massingberd, of whom Gort was later to declare that he 'was too self-satisfied to realize the damage he had done to the Army'. The outspoken Ironside not only realized, but also made his awareness plain: 'When Ironside entered the War Office as CIGS on the outbreak of war in 1939, and surveyed the Army's deficiencies in equipment, he made no

* This was not mere irascibility. In a note on Duff Cooper's *Haig* Pope once commented: 'Haig criticized not to condemn individuals nor—an even more popular device—to prove his own superiority, but to learn. Criticism is the coin in which one buys other people's experience.'

criticism of his two immediate predecessors but pointed to the portraits of Milne and Montgomery-Massingberd that hung on the wall and burst out: "Those are the two men who ought to be shot"—a verdict that was too hard on Milne.'* Such was Pope's new master: a man who preferred in an officer something he called 'loyalty' (which meant a conformist subservience) to what he denounced as 'brains' (which meant an intelligent independence of mind). There was no joy for Pope in a man who, two years earlier, had refused to read Fuller's *The Foundations of a Science of War* on the grounds that it would annoy him.

Among Pope's papers there are two documents which vividly illustrate the mental climate in which he was now immersed. The first is a paper on tank tactics which, on instruction, he had composed for his GOC and forwarded to him with obvious reluctance: 'I am afraid this is very long-winded and rather dogmatic, but the BGS had a long talk with me about tank tactics and told me to send you the gist of it.' The point, on the contrary, is that it is not long-winded but terse, and that it is only dogmatic in the sense that a statement of nursery-school platitudes is a dogma. One can observe Pope, in fact, writhing in discomfort as he tries to spell out in the simplest terminology the bare and basic essentials for an understanding of armour. 'How', one hears him saying, 'can I be even less subtle than *Field Service Regulations*?'

It was a melancholy indication of the standard of the Military Establishment at this time that the general in one of its most sought-after Commands should have had to be spoon-fed with simplifications which lay within the comprehension of a subaltern. But the second of the documents in Pope's papers explains why. This is a covering letter from Montgomery-Massingberd to the War Office, dated 22 October, 1930, with which he forwarded the Report

* Liddell Hart, *Memoirs*, Vol. I, p. 71.

of the Tank Recording Staff on the manoeuvres of the Aldershot and Southern Commands carried out the previous September. Pope had been one of the three officers in this Staff. While the General broadly accepted his experts' comments, he could not refrain from appending some of his own, and amid these lurks one which exquisitely illustrates the point of view responsible, in the end, for the deficiencies in British armour before—and after—1939. 'I am of opinion,' Montgomery-Massingberd wrote, 'that constant travelling in motor cars and tanks is largely the cause of loss of eye for ground. There is no doubt that the officer who is constantly riding about on a horse cultivates the eye for ground automatically. It is for this reason that I have been very opposed to the taking away of horses from tank battalions, and I should very much like to see them replaced.' (The previous year the Army's total budget for petrol was £27,000; for forage for horses it was £607,000.) For Pope, therefore, service under Montgomery-Massingberd was rather like sitting under a Upas tree.

Yet, say not the struggle naught availeth, as Churchill was to announce in one of his more inspired quotations:

'In front, the sun climbs slow, how slowly,
But westward, look, the land is bright.'

And a gleam did appear on the horizon, the herald of what, in the end, would prove to be a triumphant high-noon radiance. In 1929 there was issued a little pamphlet (marked 'not to be communicated either ... to the Press or to any person not authorized to receive it'). This state secret was *Mechanized and Armoured Formations*, the first official manual on armoured warfare issued by any War Office in the world. Broad was the man who drafted it. The 'Purple Primer'—so called from the colour of its covers—possibly made a greater impact than any equivalent publication, not only in England but also, and fruitfully, in Germany, where a copy arrived thanks to the traitorous act of a bungling British officer.* General Birks believed that for Pope the appearance of the 'Purple Primer' was one of the most formative events in his whole development as a man of armour.

It is easy to see why. As Liddell Hart pointed out, 'With the promulgation of this official manual the advocates of armour could feel that they had established their case in the highest court of judgement, and that their ten years' campaign had ended with a decisive verdict in their favour'. Though Broad had carefully composed the Primer to avoid giving offence, or a lever, to the diehards, Pope could read between the lines, for he was now much closer to the inner circle of the pioneers, and in any case the forty pages of text represented an explicit and authoritative registration of armour's claim to a leading place in the modern Order of Battle. Moreover, although the sun climbed slow, how slowly—since, apart from Army Council hesitation about armour, these were the days of increasing economic chaos and financial stringency—the next great step forward occurred in 1931 when, again for the first time in history, an armoured brigade was assembled and manoeuvred on Salisbury Plain. Here was demonstrated the ideal Pope had presented—'a mass of 180 tanks, marching and counter-marching, wheeling and deploying, as a single body controlled by a single voice'. Here too it became plain in the course of the exercises that horsemen had no monopoly of 'an eye for the ground'. By contrast, the unprejudiced could realize (as Guderian and others were doing in Germany) that in the conditions of a modern

* The War Office manual entitled *Mechanized and Armoured Formations* was the first summary of British thinking about the composition and handling of a mobile force. Germany acquired a copy through a certain Captain Baillie Stewart. His felony was discovered and he was confined to the Tower for treason.

battlefield tanks could move and survive where cavalry must halt and die.

Broad had produced his Primer from a firm base within the War Office, as Deputy Director in the Staff Duties department. When he departed to take over the temporary tank brigade, and then went on as BGS to Southern Command, he left an important void in Whitehall from the point of view of those who felt they had nursed the 'armoured idea' until recognition had been achieved and expansion ought to follow. To a useful extent, however, the void was filled by Pope himself, who joined SD as a GSO2 at the end of 1930 and stayed there three years. Yet he lacked the status of a Deputy Director, and apart from Pile, who was Assistant Director of Mechanization until October, 1932, there was nobody else in the corridors of decision to speak out for armour.

The fact that these were the years of Hitler's rise to power meant less than the effects of the Depression and the Disarmament Conference at Geneva. Guderian wrote of 1931 that 'we were quite convinced that the future development of our armoured troops must be directed at making them into an operationally decisive weapon'. In Britain, by 1933, there were merely four tank battalions—exactly the same number as in 1926, *with the same tanks*. But there were eighteen horsed cavalry regiments. Thus parsimony and prejudice, and the pressure of public opinion, maintained their stranglehold. In more propitious circumstances these War Office years might have been a time of great excitement and satisfaction for Pope, but never until the outbreak of war, and not always afterwards, would an armoured enthusiast find much but frustration in Whitehall. And 1931–33 was a particularly pinched period. Instead of working on stimulating plans and fine new ideas Pope was captured by routine staff duties and the petty economics of budget-balancing. This was not his style.

As he once jotted down in his note-book, under the heading 'Fools rush in where angels fear to tread':—'Yes; but they very often pull it off whilst the angels are forming Committees of Inquiry, Committees of Compromise, and Committees of Celestial Indemnity'.

By the end of 1933, however, the sun was gleaming again. In November a decision was at last taken to form 1 Tank Brigade on a permanent basis, and to give the command to Hobart, already Inspector of the Tank Corps. Few could have undertaken so taxing an extra commitment, but Hobart was Hobart. Moreover, by now he, the harshest of critics, had come to form a high regard for Pope and his abilities. The consequence was that in 1934 the 'armoured idea' burst into flame again, for Hobart's tireless, ruthless and imaginative training of the Brigade culminated in those autumn exercises which for all concerned with armour, whether in England or abroad, have become a milestone in its development. Pope himself was only a spectator on the side, though learning much from observation and discussion. He had been extricated from the War Office and now was doing the course at the Imperial Defence College, a step traditionally held to mark a man as suitable for higher promotion. It was time some came: the Lieutenant-Colonel of 1917 was still, in 1934, a Lieutenant-Colonel. And so he remained in his next appointment, for in the spring of 1935 he went out to India to take command of 5 Armoured Car Company, RTC.

But this eastern sortie only lasted a few months, for Hobart struck. A decision had been taken, understandably, to separate the posts of Commander of the Tank Brigade and Inspector of the Royal Tank Corps. In *The Tanks* Liddell Hart implies a sinister motive for this cleavage, speaking of a desire to get a difficult obstacle out of the War Office at a time when official policy was seeking to make the cavalry the dominant partner in the armoured world. Certainly this was an issue on which Hobart would and did fight to the last. But though these suspicions were justified and, if true, would have pointed to an act far less sinister than others which did occur, (the use of Hobart's divorce to damage his military career, for example), they were wrong. In India Pope received a letter from Hobart telling him that the CIGS had informed him he could no longer continue in both jobs. He could keep *either* one, but not both. Naturally, Hobart said, he was retaining command of the Tank Brigade, and he was writing now to tell Pope that he had recommended him to the CIGS as the next Inspector of the Royal Tank Corps.

CHAPTER SEVEN

THE MOBILE FORCE

Pope was not to become Inspector—except for a short while, in 1940. An officer more senior in rank and (according to Hobart) with sufficient aptitude for the job was chosen. Yet, as so often happens, a false start led to a preferable conclusion.

The reason was Italy. In October, 1935, the bombing and invasion of Abyssinia had begun, and though there was a flurry in the League of Nations about this flagrant aggression two facts soon became clear. No member of the League was prepared to use the ultimate economic sanction of denying Italy oil, and if military measures were to be required Britain would certainly have to bear the brunt. ('Not a ship, not a machine, not a man had been moved by any other member state'—Sir Samuel Hoare in the House of Commons, 19 December, 1935.) Tentative steps were therefore taken, typical of the times. *Renown* and *Hood* were sailed to Gibraltar. Malta and Aden received reinforcements, and preparations were made to set up a Mobile Force for the defence of Egypt's western frontier and, more particularly, of the airfields which had to lie as far to the west as possible because of the poor range of the available aircraft.

In all this Hobart, struggling passionately for the future of the armoured idea, saw both a danger and an opportunity. Since the projected Mobile Force would be the first ever formed by Britain as an actual instrument of war, its success—whether or not hostilities broke out—would have a profound effect on the battles he himself was continuously waging to establish armour as an integral and accepted element within the British Army. But the danger was that his cavalry-orientated superiors might select some clueless horseman to command the Force, instead of a properly trained and competent member of the Tank Corps. Yet failure could not be risked or even contemplated.

Hobart therefore moved quickly and, as it turned out, decisively. On 19 November he sent a *Personal and Private* letter to Pope in India. 'They want you brought home for a GI job about Sept next. What I am urging is that if we (RTC) reinforce Egypt you should be sent on a temporary duty to GHQ Egypt as Adviser and "Commander RTC". This would bring you half way home. It is most important for us to be strongly upheld in Egypt.' In fact he had larger issues in mind, as he affirmed on 3 December. 'I wrote you by last air-mail' [the letter is not in Pope's files] 'giving you a good many particulars: also outlining the situation—NOT the situation in Egypt, which will immediately concern you of course, as much as the big situation which will immediately affect the RTC, the Army in general, and so our prospects against the real enemy, Germany. Even if Mussolini goes berserk, this show can never be a life-or-death matter for the British Empire. But it does give us a chance of (i) getting some of our vehicles up-to-date (ii) demonstrating the RTC and checking the folly of handing over tanks and the control of mechanized formations to cavalry.'

In most of these purposes Hobart was successful, for Pope was appointed and posted to Egypt in a 'Special Appointment Class X Temporary' dating from 29 December. He was selected for the post after careful consideration by the CIGS and, as Hobart made clear to him, against a good deal of powerful lobbying by the cavalry interest. This was not surprising, for, as Hobart pointed out, eight more cavalry regiments were due to be mechanized, and 'much will be made of results of present crisis in Egypt, and great play may be made with achievements of or deductions from action of Mobile Force there'. Moreover, though the nominal commander of the miscellaneous group that was assembled around Mersa Matruh was a cavalryman, Brigadier Friend of the 11th Hussars, Hobart drafted Pope's charter with great skill, so that he was not only made responsible to the Commander-in-Chief for all matters concerning the Tank Corps in Egypt but was also empowered to take *executive* command of 'the whole or part of the RTC units in Egypt', and to issue orders direct to the RTC commanders concerned. With this lever in his hand Pope became effective commander of the Mobile Force during the Abyssinian emergency.

As an index of his concern Hobart now poured out a series of long, detailed handwritten letters by which in spite of his myriad other problems, he analyzed the capacity of Italian tanks and the tactics which might best be used against them; discussed the variant ways of handling Pope's multifarious command; kept him abreast of the shifts of military opinion in England; and ruthlessly and meticulously dissected both the weak and the efficient among the officers at home and in Eygpt. So far as possible he strove to provide Pope with the best men and the best equipment. For a staff captain, he wrote, 'I am picking you out a first-class subaltern, probably Liardet.'

As in the case of Briggs when he commanded the 3rd Armoured Car Company, Pope was again fortunate in his right-hand man, for the future Major-General H. M. Liardet, CB, CBE, DSO, a gunner who had joined the RTC in

1927, was another officer who was to serve with distinction in the Second World War and to become Colonel-Commandant of the Royal Tank Regiment. Like Briggs and Duncan, this able young man was to be struck immediately by Pope's ability. As soon as they met after Pope's arrival they went off to stay with Tim Pile, commanding the Canal Brigade, himself one of the most ardent practitioners of the idea of mobility who had done so well in the Experimental Mechanized Force in 1927. As Liardet recalled:

'We discussed the formation, role and tactics of the Force should it be called upon to operate in the Western Desert, and I, as a junior officer, was very struck with V.V.P's grasp of armoured affairs generally and his great determination and drive, so different from most senior officers at that time, whose thinking was largely dominated by the HORSE. . . . We at once started intensive training, and V.V.P's ideas of command, control and tactics in the Desert began to become clear and to dominate all our operations. We had a number of exercises in the Desert where a few years later most of us fought a real enemy, and I believe that not nearly enough credit is given to V.V.P. . . . for the basic experimental work which led to such successful handling of our Armour against the Italians in 1940–1941.'

Hobart himself is often claimed as the father of that beautiful instrument the 7th Armoured Division, which from 1940 onwards proved such a paragon. In the Division's history (*The Desert Rats*, by Major-General Verney), Hobo's work in 1938–1939 as founder and prophetic trainer of the Division is rightly emphasized, and Sir Richard O'Connor, who was shortly to defeat with its aid a whole Italian army, was not exaggerating when he declared 'it is the best trained Division I have ever seen'. Nevertheless there is much to be said for Liardet's claim about the value of Pope's work with the Mobile Force in 1936—and nothing very much has so far been said, even in Liddell Hart's *The Tanks*. The episode, perhaps because there were no hostilities, has sunk into limbo. Still, here were assembled in preparation for action the 6th Battalion RTC and the 11th Hussars from Egypt, the 1st (Light) Battalion RTC and, from England, the 1st (Light) Battalion with a Medium Tank Company. The 12th Lancers,* the 8th and 11th Hussars, an RHA Battery and the usual ancillaries also contributed to the Force. As any student will realize, most of these units were to become notable members of 7th Armoured and their practical work under Pope in 1936 was certainly a valuable preliminary. Indeed the regimental history of the 11th Hussars (*The Eleventh at War*, by Brigadier Dudley Clarke) observes: 'The desert "emergency" of 1935–36 had brought forward with impressive strides the potential fighting value of the British troops in Egypt. If the Mobile Force returned to barracks woefully conscious of the shortcomings of its equipment, at least it felt that it was now on terms with the desert and had learned the way to turn its hazards to the disadvantage of an enemy.'

Here was the snag—and the appalling truth. The Mobile Force ended by calling itself the Mobile Farce. It is often claimed that a chief value of Hitler's intrusion into Austria was its useful revelation of technical and administrative deficiencies within his mobile units. But these were as nothing compared with the horrors disclosed by the relatively small-scale mobilization of the British in 1936. There was not even a drill for sending a tank battalion abroad. When the tanks of the 1st Battalion were entrained they were locked, and the keys handed over to the Ordnance Corps. When they arrived at the docks the keys were missing, and the locks had to be forced before

* Then commanded by Richard McCreery, later Chief of Staff to Alexander at Alamein and the final commander of 8th Army in Italy.

the tanks could be moved alongside their transport ships for loading. Moreover, Hobart wrote to Pope on 30 December to warn him that the Ordnance had dumped the tanks on the quay, where they had stood uncovered for three days in pouring rain. The result was that they were awash and those with coil ignitions refused to start. 'I write to let you know that you must anticipate trouble with many of the machines.' After such a beginning it is no surprise to move on half a year and come across a letter to Lindsay of 12 July, 1936, from the capable Justice Tilly, then Chief Instructor of the RTC Central Schools. 'I saw Gross the other day, home from Egypt. The Light Bn. had 9 tanks running out of 63 and no spares. He says things are chaotic there. Vivian [sic] Pope, who I saw for a quarter of an hour the other day, says the same.'*

Among Pope's papers there is a long report by him on the mechanical efficiency of this battalion, which copiously illustrates its parlous state and observes that even were the requisite spare parts available—which they were not—'though frequent mechanical failures on the scale indicated may be tolerable in peace training, they are intolerable in war and especially in desert warfare since individual tanks cannot be left scattered in the desert to carry out repairs in the face of enemy action.' Again Pope was voicing a profound truth, whose lesson was never sufficiently learned in London, for one among the several reasons for Rommel's initial victories in the desert was precisely the mechanical unreliability of the British-built tank. Reading the long General Report he submitted one notes, for example, that tanks were sent out (to the desert) without air filters; that smoke projectors were supplied—but no ammunition; that the medium tanks had the wrong turrets, so that accumulators had to be carried 'in temporary fittings outside the turret, an entirely

* Liddell Hart, *The Tanks*, Vol. I, p. 365.

unsuitable arrangement for war'; that there were only two reserve engines available for twenty-eight medium tanks and for ninety-eight light tanks.

Only will, energy and organization could have achieved constructive training in the midst of such chaos; yet it is on record, for example, that, when the 11th Hussars finally returned to Cairo, 'perhaps for the first time since its mechanization the Regiment felt it was now equal to any calls war might bring'. As to the 1st Battalion RTC, it is worth recalling that it was its Colonel, 'Blood' Caunter, who in the winter of 1940/41 was to lead his 4th Armoured Brigade in that classic mobile operation of O'Connor's which, ending at Beda Fomm, eliminated ten Italian divisions.

Far more serious and symptomatic than any list of missing nuts and bolts was the fact that, because of a slender reinforcement from England of the few mobile units in Egypt, something like paralysis was created in the only organized armoured group which the country possessed at the time—Hobart's 1st Tank Brigade. Yet his pioneer exercises were being keenly studied in Europe and the United States, and, however much they might be disregarded or depreciated at home, they were setting a firm pattern for the future development of British armour. Of the movement of the 1st and part of the 4th Battalions to Egypt Liddell Hart wrote:

'Small as this reinforcement was, the units could only be made up to their proper strength by draining the other tank units of men and equipment. The warnings given in successive Tank Brigade reports were all too clearly confirmed. That autumn the Brigade was stripped of all its light tanks and all its wireless equipment. It was left with only the old medium tanks, and many of these were laid up for months because the RAOC was

4. Pope, at the driving wheel in the leading car, in typical desert terrain.

5. Three British Light Tanks in the desert in 1936.

6. Major-General Vyvyan Pope in 1940, shortly after he had
been appointed Director of Armoured Fighting Vehicles.

too occupied with other calls to be able to carry out repairs or provide spare parts. As a result, hardly any training could be carried out until the following spring, and then only on a much reduced basis.'

Pope's advanced detachment at Matruh was therefore nothing less than the spearhead of a national scandal. After a training session in which the Tank Brigade was worse equipped than ever before, in which lorries had to be used to represent armour, and in which wireless was so short that it was necessary to revert to visual signals, Hobart summarized the situation in the scathing opening words of his Annual Report:

The Tank Brigade has now completed three collective training sessions. It may be useful to take stock of the situation. Some years ago it was generally acknowledged that the Royal Tank Corps led the world's tank forces in the same way as the Royal Navy did the sea forces. It is admitted by the most modern tank forces on the Continent that they built themselves on the model of the Royal Tank Corps.
The Royal Tank Corps has now completely lost that lead in the matter of (a) Numbers; (b) Up-to-date Equipment—and now retains superiority, if at all, only in (c) Maintenance, Organization, and Tactical methods; and (d) Personnel.
As to *Numbers*. During these three years our potential enemies have increased enormously their tank corps. In the Royal Tank Corps no increase has taken place. . .

These melancholy words—written at a time when the Germans were already in process of creating three armoured *divisions*—remained true until the outbreak of war: true of a situation in which, even when the Blitzkrieg on the Low Countries was launched in May, 1940, the

British had not even dispatched to France the one inadequate armoured division they had so far prepared for
battle in Europe.

When the Mediterranean temperatures cooled after the
Italian conquest of Abyssinia, and the Mobile Force was
withdrawn, Pope returned to England and, in view of the
way things were to go during the next few years, it was
perhaps as well that his next appointments did not involve
him directly in the many controversies over 'the armoured
idea'. Had he been more deeply committed it is possible
that, with his strong will and passionate sense of purpose,
he might have become disillusioned and lost his zest. More
to the point is the sorry fact that by the time war had
become a reality most of those known for their pioneer
work and special aptitude for mobile operations—Hobart,
Lindsay, Broad, Pile—had all been carefully removed from
any contact with tanks. Pope, by good fortune, was just
not senior enough or prominent enough in the late 'thirties
to be Stellenbosched in this fashion.

Though he was professionally disturbed by the lack
of preparedness revealed in the last few months he was
not, at this particular point, immediately concerned about
Germany. 'Of course', he wrote to his old friend Arthur
Willis in April, 'Hitler means to absorb Austria and the
German part of Czechoslovakia and he wants to fight,
possibly in alliance with Japan, the USSR.' But he thought
that the Führer had no wish to take on the British Empire
(and in a deep sense, of course, this was true—anyway
until 1942). 'Did I tell you the story', he asked Willis, 'told
me by a certain distinguished British general who spent
some time last year visiting the German army? He was
surprised to find everywhere openly expressed the greatest
reluctance to fight the English again; the French, yes
if it must be; but the English, no. Finally he asked a
German officer why this was so. "General", the officer

replied, "we do not wish to fight you again because we are convinced that England will never be defeated until the last Scotsman has eaten his grandmother on the top of Ben Nevis".'

What did concern him, as it concerned any soldier of quality and perception in the mid-'thirties, was the low esteem in which his profession was held by his fellow-countrymen and the refusal of their Government to foster the armed services. He gathered his ideas together in a short introduction he wrote during 1936 for the 'War' section of his *Personal Anthology*. After looking back on the sacrificial spirit of which he had been an eye-witness in the First World War, and comparing it with the current apathy, he ended with a passage from Napier's history of the Peninsular War which, as one peers ahead from 1936 to 1940 and 1941, has a terrible relevance:

'And why was all this striving and blood against insurmountable difficulties? Why were men thus just sent to slaughter when the application of a just science would have rendered the operation comparatively easy? Because the English Ministers, so ready to plunge into war, were quite ignorant of its exigencies; because the English people are warlike without being military, and under the pretence of maintaining a liberty they do not possess oppose in peace all useful martial establishments. Expatiating in their schools and colleges upon Roman discipline and Roman valour they are heedless of Roman institutions; they desire like that ancient republic to be free at home and conquerors abroad, but start at perfecting their military system as a thing incompatible with the constitution which they yet suffer to be violated by every minister who trembles at the exposure of corruption. In the beginning of each war

England has to seek in blood the knowledge necessary
to insure success, and like the fiend's progress toward
Eden her conquering course is through chaos followed
by death.'

CHAPTER EIGHT

CHAOS FOLLOWED BY DEATH

'In war, as a rule, there is a shortage of something
or other. . . .'

Marshal Chuikov

Napier's words must have kept ringing in Pope's ears
during the next four years. From a sequence of important
staff appointments he was to watch his country refusing
to perfect its military system 'by the application of a just
science', and then, in France, to observe how 'in the
beginning of each war England has to seek in blood the
knowledge necessary to insure success'. 1936 was a critical
year, because in its course more than one event laid bare
the imperfections of the system. Pope was posted back
to London from Egypt in June, and thus had the opportunity of noting those deficiencies both as a commander in
the field and as a staff officer at the centre of the web in
Whitehall.

Apart from the technical weaknesses on which he
reported, the flurried preparation for possible hostilities
with Italy had revealed two deeper flaws. England had
been trapped by the emergency because the locust years
had been wasted, and no preliminary *plans* existed. The
'system' had failed. Tim Pile wrote to Liddell Hart from
the Canal Brigade in Egypt:

'Could you have been here these last four months

you would have been staggered; one always likes to think of a War Office and Admiralty so organized that, when the Prime Minister writes and says "We are likely to have trouble in 'Kismastani'—please send me the plan for dealing with it", one would walk to the pigeon-hole marked 'K', take down the plan, dust it, and send it to the Prime Minister. Of course nothing of the sort exists, and even a ridiculous show like this thwarting of ... the Italians is causing all the armed forces of the Crown endless trouble, and the Treasury will be millions of pounds poorer because there has never been a co-ordinated plan for dealing with it.'*

But it was not only the absence of plans which the Italian crisis had disclosed, it was the simple fact that the British armed forces were perilously short of both men and equipment. The least involvement in the Mediterranean, even the setting up of so small a body as Pope's Mobile Force, had immediate and disastrous consequences, as has been seen, on the training of the only armoured brigade that existed in England. And when a danger arose of simultaneous involvement in Europe, the terrible truth became plain that Britain, put at full stretch to operate in one theatre of war, was ignominiously incapable of operating in two. Yet such was the situation when, on 7 March, Hitler denounced the Locarno Pact and sent his troops into the demilitarized zone of the Rhineland. Two days later General Pownall, (at that time on the secretariat of the Committee of Imperial Defence), made an entry in his diary which neatly summarizes England's dilemma.

'On Thursday the Chiefs of Staff had an evening meeting at which they talked over the position of the three Services in the light of the present crisis. It is of course amazingly bad—partly because so much stuff is

* Liddell Hart, *Memoirs*, Vol. 1, p. 321.

in the Mediterranean, partly because our forces are *not* reconditioned (only three days before had Parliament approved!) and partly because the RAF are in the middle of their expansion scheme which naturally causes a lot of temporary disorganization ... Navally we have at home but one cruiser, 11 submarines and less than 20 destroyers. The Army, *with* mobilization, could only find two divisions and that without modern equipment—e.g., tanks—such as we have of these things being in Egypt. The RAF have some 450 first line aircraft against the German estimated strength of 770.'*

And the reality was worse than that, for, as Pope had seen, his Mobile Force had become an immobile force even without any fighting, the age or inefficiency of his tanks being quite enough to put them out of action.

On 25 June he became GSO1 in the Directorate of Military Training at the War Office—as a substantive Colonel. The DMT was Alan Brooke, and Pope was fortunate in being brought so close to a brilliant soldier with whom he was to have many and varied contacts before he died. But that aspect of military training on which he might have worked so fruitfully—training for mobile warfare—was almost non-existent, and the general conditions of training within the Army in 1936 belonged to another world. The Germans were already expanding to armoured divisions and developing the Mark III/Mark IV Panzer family which would stand them in such good stead for so many years of battle. But in England there was nothing new with which to exercise or even to anticipate. Of the three chief tanks with which the British Army were to be equipped between the outbreak of war and Pope's death in October, 1941, the Crusader and the Valentine were

* *Chief of Staff*, the Diaries of Lieut-Gen Sir Henry Pownall (Leo Cooper, 1973), Vol. 1, p. 105.

not even at the drawing-board stage in 1936, while the Matilda was only in process of evolution.

Alan Brooke himself, a gunner without particular experience of mobile operations, had no great passion for 'the new idea' about armour and was, indeed, inclined to resist the ardour of its enthusiasts. He was not a man to be converted by prophets. There was no significance in his becoming for a short while, in 1938, commander of England's first Mobile Division, except that he was appointed to keep out either a cavalryman or an officer from the Royal Tank Corps—and a good thing too, since the first choice of the CIGS for this critical post was the Commandant of the Equitation School at Weedon! Yet his instincts were sound, for, though he was no man of armour, he believed—or came to believe—in the primacy of one point which was to escape many British armoured commanders, a point which Pope himself had grasped and which he clutched to the end. The DMT and his GSO1 both saw that as a matter of principle tanks must be used *en masse* and not frittered away in small numbers—the endemic habit of British commanders. Brooke only held one exercise with the Mobile Division, but the doctrines he laid down at its end were: (1) that the division must be used as a formation and never split up; (2) that it should not be used piecemeal to support a break-in by the infantry, which was the job of Army Tank Brigades; (3) that after the break-in its task was to go wide and deep and prevent the battle becoming static.

All of this was entirely in tune with Pope's own thinking, though he was to see little of it applied, except by the Germans, in his lifetime. Such harmony of thought was important during Pope's period at the War Office, for Brooke's highly-geared personality could not comfortably tolerate those who did not fit in. But the next few years would show how Pope had fitted. And indeed nothing would have given his own sardonic mind greater pleasure than to have been with Colonel Peter Dunphie (who later became Military Assistant to Brooke when he was CIGS). One day in 1941 Dunphie was attending Brooke, then Commander-in-Chief Home Forces, on a large exercise in which one Corps was defending the South Tyne while another, with an armoured division under command, was to force a crossing. Brooke was keenly interested in the employment of the armour.

> *Brooke:* 'And where is the armoured division?'
> *Corps Cdr:* 'I have got the tanks deployed across the whole front. They are to deliver a series of pin-prick attacks in order to find weak spots in the enemy defences.'
> *Brooke:* 'You have in your hand a sledge-hammer and not a bloody pin-cushion.'

The immediate removal of the Corps Commander from his post, Colonel Dunphie recalls,* was then arranged.

The fact was that the Army Council and the main climate of military opinion were still conditioned by the values of the First World War. More perceptive than the politicians, the keener minds on the staff did at least appreciate that a European conflict would compel Britain to land more than token troops on the Continent, but the kind of expeditionary force envisaged was always of the conventional infantry pattern. Thus there was neither encouragement nor stimulus for the man with fresh ideas; for those who, like Pope, placed their trust in speed of thought and speed of action an office in Whitehall was a kind of grave. It is significant that Wavell, under whom Pope was soon to serve and who, at that time, was one of the most brilliant and original trainers of troops in the

* Letter to the author.

country, turned down in May, 1936, the offer of the Directorate of Military Training which then went to Alan Brooke. 'The job had no attraction whatever,' he wrote. 'I knew I should not see eye to eye with the CIGS as to how the Army should be trained, and anyway the DMT could exercise comparatively little influence, and there was still no money and no equipment ... I begged to be excused, quite firmly.' His no less brilliant friend Jock Burnett-Stuart replied, 'You are well out of it. It consists mainly of teaching several grandmothers to suck eggs.'

Service under these three exceptional men would, as it happened, occupy Pope until and after the outbreak of war, for at the end of March, 1938, he was appointed Brigadier, General Staff, Southern Command, where General Burnett-Stuart was just completing his reign before retirement. In April he was succeeded by Wavell, whom the reforming Hore-Belisha had brought back from Palestine as part of his policy of filling key posts with able and younger men. Pope acted as right-hand man to Wavell for a year, until he departed to take up the new office of Commander-in-Chief, Middle East, and was followed by Alan Brooke. There was not only an immense stimulus to be derived from working closely with two of the out-standing soldiers of their generation. There was also, for Pope, a much more vivid sense of reality, in that Southern Command was traditionally the producer of one of the first Corps to sail in any Continental Expeditionary Force. Moreover, it was a convention that the GOC Southern Command would become the GOC of the operational Corps which he had fathered—and Wavell was, indeed, notified that this would be the case. The further assumption, therefore, was that the GOC would take with him into action his senior staff officers, and thus Pope could reasonably assume (as turned out to be the case) that if his general went to war he would be at his side.

The historian Sir Charles Petrie saw a good deal of Pope at this time and from his recollections it is clear that the devil within had not subsided. The cavalier student at the Staff College existed inside the 'responsible' Brigadier, and in spite of his single arm Pope would still drive his car at a fearsome rate; when he got angry with the driver in front of him, as he was liable to do, he was still capable of reducing his passengers to terror and a need for stiff whiskies. But what chiefly impressed Petrie about Pope was the range of his interests and reading. A fluent talker himself, he found that he never needed to halt to explain his allusions. When they took their children on a visit to Stonehenge, for example, he observed that, in a furious argument with the guide, whom Pope held to be wrong, the Brigadier overwhelmed his opponent by asking him if he had read the latest pamphlet on the subject, which Pope, unlike the guide, had studied.

Petrie also noticed how confidently Wavell (whom he also knew well) relied on Pope as his BGS. 'It was possible for a commander to lose himself in a welter of detail; this fate Wavell avoided by restricting his paper work to the minimum and spending as much time as he could out and about his widespread Command, looking at formations and units.'* Pope kept the shop tidy. And though, as Wavell complained, even at this late date, with the threat from Hitler daily looming larger, there were no man-oeuvres on any large scale, so that he had no proper practice in command in the field, nevertheless it was not in Wavell's nature to stagnate. As when he was a divisional commander, so now it was under his aegis that some of the more forward-looking exercises of the day were carried out, and Pope, of course, had much to learn from his involvement in them.

They were not always successful, but the point of an

* John Connell, *Wavell, Scholar and Soldier*, p. 199.

exercise in new techniques is to learn from mistakes. Neither the Experimental Mechanized Force in the 'twenties, nor the Tank Brigade in its tentative manoeuvres, had avoided error; and from Pope's standpoint what mattered was that under Wavell he was concerned with growth and the future rather than with the outworn and the past. Shortly after Wavell took over, for example, an invasion exercise was held near Dartmouth which was, in a sense, a trial run for Normandy's D Day in 1944. The infantry were supplied by the 9th Brigade, commanded by one Brigadier Bernard Montgomery, and the landings were watched by the skeleton staff of the newly formed ISTDC (Inter-services Training and Development Centre) which was to pioneer many of the methods later employed in Combined Operations. Wavell commented that 'It was a pitiful exposition of our complete neglect of landing operations. There was *one* so-called landing craft, an experimental one made many years before and dug out of some scrap-heap for this exercise, in which I rather think it sank. For the rest, the troops landed in open row-boats as they had done for the last 200 years and more.'*

The following spring there was another exercise which Wavell managed to have arranged for careful study of the support of land by air forces. It seems inconceivable that this was an almost totally disregarded subject in March, 1939, a few months before the *Luftwaffe* supplied very practical demonstrations in Poland. But so it was. Wavell judged that the exercise 'showed conclusively that the RAF had given little or no thought to the problem of ground operations'. It was good for Pope to be living in a circle where such things seemed to matter, good to be in the constant company of a man who that year gave at

---

* Not that the Army was always better off than the Navy. Many of the Bren-gun carriers in the 1939 Southern Command manoeuvres were inscribed: 'Not to be used in action. Mild steel only. Not armour plate.'

Cambridge his classic Lees-Knowles lectures on *Generals and Generalship*—those shrewd and stimulating lectures which Rommel used to carry around with him in the desert. And there was another affinity—the private anthology which Pope had been assembling for years has much in common with *Other Men's Flowers*.

Unfortunately he did not share to the same extent the particular passion of his next master. At the end of July Wavell departed for the Middle East, having handed over to Alan Brooke, who in turn had handed over to Tim Pile as GOC Anti-Aircraft Command. The dedication to ornithology which is so surprising an aspect of Brooke's personality was not a bond between himself and his new BGS. However, Brooke had already taken the measure of Pope in their Whitehall days together, and when, at the beginning of September, he set up the mobilization headquarters of 2 Corps at Salisbury, he kept on Pope as the Brigadier General Staff with whom he would go to war.*

Their problems were enormous. In the two divisions which constituted the Corps half the men were reservists. 'Neither had had any divisional or even brigade training, and their infantry, who had learnt their battle-drill with marking-flags, had only been issued with machine-guns in the past year. Their few tanks were without even such elementary equipment as wireless sets, while the artillery's new 25-pounder guns were still in process of issue and the gunners unpractised in their use.'† Out of this thing of threads and patches, the best that Britain could produce, Alan Brooke and his Chief of Staff, Vyvyan Pope, must evolve a fighting instrument. It could be done; that it was done Brooke's Corps proved in its famous defence of the Allied flank outside Dunkirk. But in September, 1939, the

* Pope in fact designed the badge of the Corps—a salmon athwart a 'brook'. Alan Brooke was a dedicated fisherman.
† Arthur Bryant, *The Turn of the Tide*, p. 50.

need was for time—time to equip, time to learn, time to knit together. A few days previously Montgomery had taken over 3 Division, one of the two in the Corps, and in his *Memoirs* he has written a scathing and unforgettable account of its unpreparedness.

Only the fighting man can know how essential non-combatants are for his success. A Corps is a complicated and sophisticated instrument, which can only be controlled by good communications and sustained by orderly administration. But Pope recorded that even before Brooke began to mobilize 2 Corps for passage to France he reported to the War Office that it would be unfit for active service without at least a month's training, and one reason was its communications. The Corps Signals unit was to be composed of Territorials, still deficient as to some 50% of their tradesmen. Pope remembered 'The War Office's rigid determination to remove the Corps Signals from their training place on the Plain in order to send them back to their appointed places of mobilization. This decision meant a loss of ten invaluable days' training and appeared to be quite unnecessary. At first it was said that the unit must go back to receive its mobilization equipment; but when we proposed to bring the equipment to the unit, the ground was changed and we were told that the movement tables were made out from the drill halls and could not be altered.'* As for administration, there were no trained clerks. 'Our senior clerk was a QMS of doubtful ability, and we promoted a corporal to QMS and two privates to sergeant, while the privates posted to us could not type and knew little or nothing of clerical duties.'

There was some consolation in a visit from Lord Gort and Pownall, his Chief of Staff, before they departed for

---

* This and quotations in the following chapter come from a set of notes made by Pope after his return from France in December, 1939.

France. The Commander-in-Chief made it plain that he appreciated the need for extending training in 2 Corps and that this was understood by General Gamelin under whom the BEF would serve. A few days later Philip Neame VC (Pownall's Deputy) came down to Salisbury after a visit to France. 'He divulged in some detail the plan for our assembly in an area far removed from the front, and for our move from the assembly area to a concentration area behind the front, where, he said, we should train for a month or so before taking over a portion of the frontier defences which, in the meantime, would be held by 1 Corps.'

But all this was moonshine. Brooke and Pope crossed to Cherbourg on 29 September and drove to GHQ. 'Here the Corps Commander saw Philip Neame who told him that the plans were altered and that 2 Corps would have to go into the line direct from the assembly area. The collapse of Poland had caused the French High Command to fear that German operations might start a good deal earlier on the western front than was previously expected and the BEF was required to take over its sector as quickly as possible. The Corps Commander again said that 2 Corps was not fit to operate yet, to which Philip Neame could only say that the plan was altered.' The argument grew so heated—and Brooke in argument could be white hot— that Pope tactfully slipped away to consult the Intelligence branch. All he could gather was that 'there was no definite information that a German attack was impending, but precautions had to be taken'. Pope had heard that one before.

CHAPTER NINE

THE RECKONING

'Truth will come to light'
Shakespeare, *The Merchant of Venice*

Four years in the trenches of the Western Front had taught Pope to view with pessimism any optimistic predictions of the General Staff. Now he was back again, and the pattern proved to be the same. He and Brooke moved their ill-prepared 2 Corps forward into its stations on the French frontier and started the essential processes of digging, wiring, and manufacture of pill-boxes, an operation for which the French on their flanks lent little inspiration. 'They seemed listless, bored and ill-cared for.'* Unlike Gort, however, who seemed to be in a state of euphoria, neither Brooke nor his fellow commander of 1 Corps, Dill, were under any illusions. On 15 October Brooke described in his diary, 'The whole country dressed in their Sunday best and apparently sitting on a volcano'. That very night he and Pope learned that a German attack through Belgium was anticipated at any moment by the French High Command. The British staff had got it wrong. We now know, of course, that throughout the winter of 1939–40 Hitler made a series of specific plans for launching an assault in the west, any one of which might have been implemented had it not been for the weather or some other unpredictable factor.

* Arthur Bryant, *The Turn of the Tide*, p. 62.

One of the most definite of these plans was very soon announced by the Führer—on 27 October. This was the day when, in the face of strong opposition from his generals, he instructed his High Command that preparations should be made to start Operation YELLOW—the invasion of the Low Countries—on 12 November. Only an adverse meteorological report prevented Hitler from releasing his Panzers and Gamelin from ordering the British forward in a headlong advance to the Scheldt. Brooke, who was now proud of his 2 Corps, dreaded the idea of having to sacrifice it in so ill-considered a fashion—especially as Pope had noted that when Neame came down to Salisbury to brief them he had stated that, 'In the event of the Germans invading Belgium and the Belgians asking for our assistance, Gamelin was determined not to engage in an encounter battle'. Fortunately the bad weather continued, and intensified during December.

These were taxing days for Pope. A Chief of Staff certainly carries a less personal responsibility than his master, but in many respects, and particularly in a theatre of war, he is the chief executive who keeps the whole machine in operation. 2 Corps was simultaneously training Territorials fresh from their drill halls, preparing defences, improvising for the lack of equipment, and trying to blend in one properly functioning organism many thousands of men who had previously never served together in the same formation. Readers of the *Alanbrooke Diaries* well know with what an intensity of nervous energy he threw himself into his task. Both the character of his master and his own perfectionism drove Pope hard.* In December he returned to England to take command of 3 Armoured

---

* As Brooke understood. On 12 January he wrote to Pope from France: 'I want first and foremost to thank you once again for all your invaluable help in getting the 2 Corps started and established out here. It meant a lot of hard pioneering work for you. . . . I miss you very much and feel very lost without you.'

Brigade in East Anglia, where he was greeted by an old friend, Nigel Duncan, who was the Brigade Major. Duncan observed that, 'He was more abstemious than ever and also took more pills or tablets. I think he suffered from acute indigestion but although I think he was often in acute pain it never daunted him for a minute—he was a little more irritable and it behoved one to walk very warily when he was in that mood.' The nervous dyspepsia which had dogged Pope in one way or another ever since his first war in France was a ready index to his stress and over-strain.

As he travelled round a wintry East Anglia getting to know his new Brigade Pope felt the shadow of his predecessor, for Justice Tilly was a well-known figure in the Tank Corps. Any man who had carried out front-line reconnaissance for his armour at the battle of Cambrai on the back of a mule was bound to be legendary; in addition, Tilly had been closely involved in the peacetime struggles for the 'armoured idea'. Yet Duncan recalled, 'Justice Tilly was a jolly good Brigadier, but Vyvyan could run rings round him and all the units of the formation very quickly realized that they were indeed under entirely new management. He was quick as light, got hold of all the problems in a flash, and terrified me by driving his staff car in a snow-and-icebound land at the most tremendous speed. In fact he was completely clued up on all aspects and entirely understood the troubles that units were having with the A13 cruiser tanks which had just been issued to us. These were incomplete in many items. V.V. was completely methodical and maintained lists and tables himself so that he knew exactly what the situation was. He used a small ring-back notebook covered inside with pages of his spidery writing. He wrote the most awful hand and couldn't bear to be asked what a word was. Rumour had it that when he went in for the Staff College exam he headed every page with the caption, "Bad handwriting due to physical disability." It was needed!'

The irony and the tragedy of the British situation in 1939 and 1940, for men like Pope and Duncan and Tilly who had devoted many years to the study of armoured warfare, was that at a time when a powerful German attack was daily expected in France they, the experts, had no efficient weapons ready to their hands. The sorry truth is comprised in the story of the A13 cruiser tank whose shortcomings and shortages Pope was now registering in his left-handed calligraphy. After War Office lethargy and Treasury parsimony had at last been overcome and, in the latter 'thirties, some effort had been made to press forward a British tank programme, the A13, commissioned from the Nuffield organization, was rushed into production within two years of initiating the design. This halving of the normal time-span produced inevitable consequences. Many unforeseen difficulties arose, and when tanks finally began to reach the troops—including Pope's 3 Armoured Brigade —their mechanical performance was still unreliable, a record of inefficiency which the A13 passed on to the useless Covenanter and the more successful but still inadequate Crusader. You can train men, but not weapons.*

And the moment of truth was now approaching. In mid-April Pope was promoted to Inspector of the Royal Armoured Corps (the Tank Corps and the cavalry having been merged under this single head in 1939). This was the post for which Hobart had tried to obtain Pope as his successor in 1935, though the responsibilities were now vastly extended. But it was short-lived, for he was soon nominated to join Gort's staff at HQ, BEF, as Adviser on Armoured Fighting Vehicles. Then, as he noted in his diary for 10 May, 'At 8 am I switched on the wireless and

* Nor, indeed, designers of genius. The death of John Carden of Vickers in an air crash in 1935 was disastrous for the development of armour.

heard that Germany had at 4 am that day invaded Holland and Belgium. At last the gloves are off. I decided to cross over to France at once ... instead of waiting till the selected date of the 15th.'

Pope's performance in the battle which he now joined did him much credit, for though his post as Adviser was by definition non-operational he contrived, in an entirely voluntary fashion, to get usefully involved in the heart of the fighting. The instinct which had always drawn the young officer of the North Staffs into no-man's-land was still alive. And not only was he theoretically restricted to the rear as Gort's Adviser; there was not, in fact, very much for him to advise about. On the day the Germans struck, the British Order of Battle only showed the 12th Lancers with their armoured cars, the four lightly equipped regiments of Divisional Cavalry (the 4th/7th Dragoons, 5th Inniskillings, 13th/18th and 15th/19th Hussars), and the two regiments of the 1st Light Armoured Reconnaissance Brigade (the Fife and Forfar, and the East Riding Yeomanry). The only armour of any substance was in Douglas Pratt's 1st Army Tank Brigade with its 4th and 7th Battalions of the RTR (Britain's first and only Armoured Division, though it finally reached France in bits and pieces, was never engaged in the main actions east of the Somme which preceded the evacuation from Dunkirk). In any case, once Gort had taken the decision to conduct the battle from his advanced Command Post, and sever himself from most of his staff, it would not have been easy for Pope to influence the C-in-C directly; his communications were, in fact, always with Gort's subordinates. In so far as he had an empire, therefore, it was neither very large nor very easy to administer. This became clear when on 12 May Pope reported at Wahagnies, then the location of Gort's Command Post, and moved on to 2 Corps at Sottingen, where he found that the officer supposed to be co-ordinating the cavalry units along the front had not yet got in touch with his regiments. 'Suggested he should do so without delay. As I am not a commander, I have to walk delicately in matters like that'.

But a much more important point arose, which illustrated the difficulty of bringing expert advice to bear on senior officers who had habitually failed to acquaint themselves with the limitations, as well as the possibilities, of armour. As part of the great sweep forward of the BEF it was planned to move 1 Army Tank Brigade eastwards. 'I am not at all happy about the move of 1 Army Tk Bde. If—and it is a big if—all goes well, then there is nothing more to be said except to ensure that tactically it is soundly placed and the General Staff seem confident of this. But if things go wrong, it will be the devil to get out. I sounded Robert Bridgeman* on this before I left Arras† and he fully appreciated the situation and promised to represent it to the CGS. On arrival at Wahagnies I raised the question again, but was gently snubbed. We are certainly going to fight in front of Brussels, I was told, and that was that. I can only hope the GS is right. They can scarcely realize that A11s and A12s are not designed for and are not mechanically capable of long marches on their tracks'. Pope's intuition was correct, for after this forward move (which led to no action) the Tank Brigade was pulled back again, to take part at last in the famous battle at Arras on 21 May—but the journeying had played such havoc with the tracks and other parts of the tanks' mechanism that many were *hors de combat* before the battle even began. Pope calculated on the 20th that the Brigade had covered 160 miles in five days, (the true figure was nearer 120), and that in consequence about 25% of its

---

* Major-General the Viscount Bridgeman, KBE, CB, DSO, MC was at this time a senior Staff Officer at GHQ.
† GHQ, BEF.

original strength had been dissipated by road marching. Such is the price paid by officers who misuse infantry tanks designed to move short distances on the battlefield, and by countries whose parsimony or lack of foresight fail to supply essential items like tank-transporters.

This desperate switching about of the only effective piece on the board would, of course, have been less necessary if even one armoured division with its further-ranging cruiser tanks had been present with the BEF. In fact plans were made to establish 1 Armoured Division in the forward area as soon as it arrived, though circumstances and the speed of the German advance prevented it from even crossing the Somme. Pope was much exercised over these plans, for he diagnosed a lack of purpose in the Divisional command. On the 13th he noted: 'B. arrives this evening. He is very anxious that the Division should concentrate forward, if necessary unit by unit, and be prepared to fight as it comes in. Too much dilly-dally and soft living has enervated the tissues of 1 Armd. Div., but at heart it is sound enough and has much more dash than its commander gives it credit for.' The intention was to concentrate the Division north and south of the road Ninove–Brussels. Pope felt that there was 'too much safety first' in the attitude of the divisional representative who 'would like to concentrate at Boulogne or Calais and move up quietly; very nice if we were not engaged in a decisive battle'.

His diary entry for the next day, the 14th, begins: 'Stayed at Arras all day in an attempt to get into the picture and catch up with office work.' As Adviser, Pope only had a minute set-up at GHQ but there was one inestimable advantage, for his GSO1 was Raymond Briggs, once his Adjutant in his Armoured Car Company in Egypt. With Briggs as a firm and reliable base, Pope felt free to travel around the various Corps and Divisional headquarters to see for himself what was happening to the armour. This was not always easy.

'The road was packed with Belgian transport withdrawing as rapidly as possible, and more rapidly than possible, and as H.K., the driver, has a poor night-vision, worse than mine, the drive is disturbing. After about five miles of agitation the inevitable happens and we have a head-on collision with a Belgian car driven at high speed on the wrong side of the road. Both cars are wrecked, but nobody, strangely enough, seriously injured. A RAOC Recovery Officer helped me to clear the road and then volunteered to take me on my way. He is very willing but is also very short-sighted, and the journey, down the crowded main road covered with three lines of panic-stricken Belgians whose heavy lorries stop for nothing, is not soothing, especially as our car is a light Austin.'

Nevertheless, during the next few days Pope was to show that his principle of 'control from the front' was invaluable. On the morning of the 17th the Army Tank Brigade was under command of 1 Corps. Douglas Pratt recorded how a message arrived from Corps, 'ordering them to turn about and move on Enghien to deal with German tanks that had broken through at Hal. The column reversed while the Brigade Commander drove ahead to verify the situation. He found the HQ of the right brigade of the 5th Division, commanded by the then Brigadier Dempsey*, who was perfectly satisfied with their situation and had heard nothing of German tanks! The column was halted, but not before some fifteen miles had been covered to no purpose whatsoever. At this time, Brigadier Pope

---

* Later Lieut-General Sir Miles Dempsey and commander in 1944 of the British Second Army in NW. Europe.

arrived from GHQ. He was extremely angry at the 1 Corps order.'

In fact, Pope had already made a decision as soon as he heard how the Tank Brigade was being shuttled about, and had immediately arranged with GHQ to have it removed from the Command of 1 Corps and brought into reserve, where it would be less likely to be maltreated. The railways were now abandoned by their staffs, and it was precisely the kind of useless road-work to which tank-tracks were now being exposed which would diminish the power of the British armour when it was truly needed. Next day Pope followed the progress of the Brigade and found its head in the middle of Tournai, whose streets had been blocked by a heavy air raid. The officer at the head of the column 'was in a state of excitement and had to be calmed'.

On the 19th Pope evolved a new role for himself—that of Horatius. In the morning he went north to the 1 Corps area to have a look at the armed reconnaissance brigades on that front, but he discovered that there was considerable anxiety about the blowing of the bridges over the Escaut. 'I, ill-advisedly, volunteered to go up and see that the bridges were not blown too soon—or too late.' When he came to the bridge between Tournai and Antoing:

'I asked the young officer in command if he had any troops guarding the bridge so as to prevent it from being rushed. "Oh, yes, Sir", he said brightly, and pointed to a sentry at one end of the bridge. "Have you anyone in front to give you a warning of the enemy's approach?" I asked. "Oh, yes, Sir", he said again, and indicated a sentry standing on the far side of the bridge. I suggested that his dispositions were not fool-proof against enemy armoured cars, and ordered him to put sentries well out so that he could get very early information of a German advance, and to make quite sure that the RE were in position to blow the bridge instantaneously in the event of trouble.'

At Antoing itself things were even worse. Defence and then destruction of these Escaut bridges was vital for safeguarding the British withdrawal: yet here, where it was possible to approach unseen from the east to within 50 yards of the bridge, there were neither sentries nor patrols on the further bank. Pope seized a squadron commander and three light tanks of the East Riding Yeomanry, which were retiring across the river, and pushed them back to form a screen. 'The squadron commander, who had not been in touch with the enemy that day, disliked this thoroughly, especially when at 3 pm we could hear the explosions of other bridges being blown up to the north and south of us, but I told him that I proposed to hang on to the crossing for at least another hour. I did a short reconnaissance myself on foot, but did not like to go too far as the E. Ridings were rather jumpy and I did not want either to get shot up by them or to mask their fire.' Contrary and confusing orders now began to arrive, and at 5.30, as no British troops had withdrawn over the bridge since three o'clock, Pope on his own initiative gave the order for the bridge—or bridges; there were four of them—to be blown.

He went next to the bridge south of Tournai, a large and important crossing prepared for demolition with three tons of explosive. But here too there was no covering party and no orders. The sapper officer in charge was eager to blow, but Pope restrained him, and sure enough a large party of infantry from 3 Brigade and one light tank of the Dragoons came over shortly afterwards. There were enemy on the way, but Pope set about organizing a party to stalk and ambush them so that he could hold open the bridge as long as possible. Soon, however, it became clear that the strength of the opposition was too great, and at 8.10 pm he ordered the bridge to be blown. 'I was very sick at heart in the thought that possibly some of our troops had been left out, and could not help wondering whether more resolute action on my part might not have driven off the Boche and retained a bridgehead.' Still, he might have calmed his conscience by asking how much the day's activities fell within the normal scope of a GHQ Adviser on Armoured Fighting Vehicles.

There followed an operation in which Pope was able to perform to the full his part as a tank general—the famous British 'counter-attack' at Arras on 21 May: it will be seen that his contribution was considerable, though this is not normally recognized in accounts of the battle. The situation on the 19th and in the early hours of the 20th was that a German spearhead—Rommel's 7 Panzer Division —had reached Cambrai, about 25 miles to the south-east of Arras. On the morning of the 20th Pope was told that two infantry divisions, 5 and 50, were being placed under command of Major-General Franklyn, together with the Tank Brigade, to take the offensive south of Arras, and he himself was instructed to get the tanks on the move from their harbour at Orchies, some 30 miles away, down to the Vimy Ridge. The aim of the attack, Pope noted at the time, was 'to support the garrison in Arras by clearing the roads south of that town and cutting off the German communications from the east, and to occupy the River Scarpe east of Arras gaining contact with the French on the left. The French Cavalry Corps were to co-operate in the attack.'

Its scope, in other words, was that of a limited, spoiling offensive-defensive operation. So it was certainly understood by all those involved. Rommel, as we know from his *Papers*, was thrown off balance by its impact and wrote of 'very powerful armoured forces' thrusting out of Arras, while a wave of nervous reaction passed through the German High Command right up to Hitler himself. In fact the Tank Brigade could only raise seventy-four operational tanks, of which only sixteen were the strong Mark II Matildas. (It was the inability of their guns to penetrate the latter's armour which particularly shocked the Germans.) Nor, in the end, were two British infantry divisions involved. When the time came, no more than a couple of tired *battalions* of 50 Division could be raised for the assault. All this has to be seen in the larger strategical context, for these were the days when Weygand's fantasy of a great joint pincer-movement by the British from the north and the French from the south was being ventilated as the last desperate attempt to cut off the German Panzers. The fantasy, of course, never became fact; but while, as has been seen, the Arras 'counter-attack' had never more than a local purpose, it came to be visualized in the high command, and as far back as London, as the heart of the British contribution to the Weygand Plan. It is a matter of some historical importance, therefore, to observe that in Pope's detailed contemporary diary there is no hint at all that these larger issues were involved. As he, Franklyn and the other men on the spot saw it, they were simply and hectically involved in a private local affray.

Pope got to Orchies about midday on the 20th and ordered the armour forward. Refugee columns, marching troops and air attacks slowed the rate of progress, and the last tank did not arrive until five o'clock next morning. However:

'In the late afternoon I went down the Lens–Arras road to see the Brigade into harbour on Vimy Ridge. The move was being watched by a German reconnaissance plane, so I halted the front of the column near Avion, just south of Lens, and told them not to move on till dusk to Vimy. I then went in search of Pratt and/ or 'Q' Martel.* I was told they were on Vimy Ridge, so I went up there. The place was littered with transport and troops, but a prolonged search failed to find either commander. As I had made up my mind to come away, three Messerschmitts came over flying very low and began to machine-gun the ridge and the troops indiscriminately.'

Fortunately Pope did manage to contact General Franklyn, and found him reasonably confident but sharing the French view that 'no large-scale operation could take place before the day after tomorrow, i.e., 22 May.' In his journeyings that day Pope had fallen in with a conference of the French Cavalry Corps where he had heard the same pessimistic views expressed. He now quickly disabused Franklyn, telling him the C-in-C expected an attack on the morrow, and returned to the Command Post at Wahagnies to report. The Deputy Chief of Staff, Oliver Leese, was horrified at the idea of delay and, 'after discussion with the French, who showed little signs of wishing to accelerate matters, and with Franklyn on the telephone, decided to attend a special conference at Franklyn's HQ at 6 am, 21 May.' After an hour's rest Pope picked up Leese at 3.30 am, and together they met Franklyn at 5.15 in his Vimy HQ, where it was agreed that the attack should begin at two that afternoon.

When zero hour came Pope followed the tanks down to the crossings of the Scarpe, just west of Arras. They were moving alone. The infantry were late, but, rather than postpone, Martel had sent the armour on ahead. Its artillery support was also delayed, and promised assistance

* Commander of 50 Division and in charge of the attack.

from the air never materialized. Nevertheless, when Pope climbed up to the Arras racecourse, from which he had a panoramic view of the battlefield, he was not disappointed. 'There was a slight haze which made detailed observation difficult, but it did my heart good to see the resolute manner in which the Brigade went into action. There was a good deal of machine-gun and anti-tank gun fire, more than I expected, but the tanks pushed on without faltering and as they passed the fire was subdued.' Pope now crossed the Scarpe and went on to the village of Dainville, where Martel and Douglas Pratt were to set up an HQ. As they had not arrived he set off on foot into the battle-field. Here he found one of the tank battalion commanders 'in a state of some excitement, having completely lost himself. His Battalion and he himself had come in too far to the left, and I formed the impression that he was not in control of his unit at all.'

Pope pushed the Colonel forward and then made contact with the infantry battalion commander, whose men were coming up at last. They were tired, and still lagging three miles behind the armour. Pope urged the infantry on, since he had discovered from the tank officers he had questioned that German resistance was being smashed, as the enemy anti-tank guns were proving useless against the well-clad Matildas. Then, making his way back to GHQ, he came across Pratt who was completely out of touch, even by wireless and ordered him to close up to the front. His verdict on all he had seen was :'I cannot but think that in this action the commanders generally were too far back. In an armoured action it is essential that commanders should be well up to take immediate advantage of fleeting opportunites and to deal with sudden changes in the situation'.

The attack had done astonishingly well, but there was not much left of the British armour. Next morning Pope was given a delicate mission by Oliver Leese—to visit Franklyn, ascertain the situation, and tell him, *and him alone*, to have in mind a plan for withdrawal in case it should be ordered that night. Returning to report that Franklyn insisted on discussing such a plan with his staff, Pope was now told that 'any withdrawal was out of the question and that Franklyn must hold on to Arras'. As Pope knew that Franklyn was hard-pressed, he made Oliver Leese give him the new instructions personally on the telephone. He then returned to Arras. It was a quieter day, but he was active throughout it in helping Franklyn to stabilize the situation. When he returned to Wahagnies in the evening, however, 'another crisis had arisen'. The intention had been to move the Command Post to Haze-brouck; Gort had departed for Hazebrouck; German tanks were now reported on its outskirts; how to rescue the C-in-C? As Pope was thought to be good at finding his way by night, he was despatched with orders to drive with headlights full on. He had a sensational journey—often shot at and once arrested—to find on his arrival that Gort was in bed and all was well.

Meanwhile an entirely new area of operations was emerging over which Pope was unfortunately to have no influence—unfortunately, because the authority of his presence might well have had a significant effect. On the 20th Briggs had visited him at Wahagnies to report that 1st Armoured Division was disembarking south of the Somme and that he was flying there to assist them. That statement requires some expansion.

No 'Division' arrived in France, in the sense of a complete and fighting-fit formation. It was a truncated and ill-equipped force which, under Major-General Evans, passed through Cherbourg to assemble piecemeal in the Tank Training Area at Pacy, south of the Seine. All its infantry and artillery support had gone to implement

Churchill's edict that 'Calais should be fought to the death'. To Calais also had gone one of its tank battalions, 3 RTR. Of the 284 tanks which reached France only 150 were cruisers, recently issued and short of wireless, sights and anti-tank shot: the rest were light tanks.

It was to this unready conglomeration—so different from the Panzer divisions—that Briggs on the 21st brought orders to secure the bridges over the Somme (south of which the Germans had already established bridgeheads). Evans' instructions were intensified on the 23rd to read: 'Immediate advance of whatever elements of your division are ready is essential. Action at once may be decisive; tomorrow may be too late.' That such a plan was wholly impractical is another story: what is important for the biography of Vyvyan Pope is that an error has crept into the records which seriously reflects on the judgement of himself and his staff.

The *Official History** states unequivocally that these orders were supported by an affirmation from Briggs to Evans that to the north of the Somme only 'the mangled remains of six Panzer divisions' were in action, together with other details suggesting that the cavalier advance of 1st Armoured Division across the river would have little to fear on the other side. This was a monstrous misreading of the situation, for by now no less than ten powerful Panzer divisions had thrust between the Somme and the main body of the BEF. Yet the legend persists, for in 1973 Major Gregory Blaxland in his *Destination Dunkirk*† wrote of how 'a strange rash of delusion touched GHQ', and how by the reckoning of the Armoured Section the theory of 'the mangled remains' was circulated. (The Armoured Section means the office of the Adviser on Armoured Fighting Vehicles—i.e. Pope and Briggs.)

* *The War in France and Flanders*, p. 255.
† Gregory Blaxland, *Destination Dunkirk*, Kimber, 1973.

But neither Pope nor Briggs had been responsible for so misleading GHQ and General Evans. The error in the *Official History* arises from a simple but crucial misinterpretation. Briggs did indeed issue a 'Situation Report' on 23 May, as from Pope's office, which contained the false information about the German armour. This, however, was clearly entitled 'as known at GQG on night 22/23 May 40'. In other words, it was a summary of intelligence issued by the headquarters, or *Grand Quartier Général*, of the *French*, and was received by Briggs from the British mission to General Georges under whose direct command 1 Armoured Division had been placed. Moreover, General Briggs confirmed to the author on 18 February, 1974, that 'when handing this over to Evans I was careful to explain that this was what the French General Headquarters had issued and that I had no knowledge of what Gort's HQ knew of the situation in detail.' For GQG the *Official History* had read GHQ.

The subsequent story of the Armoured Division is a classic example of using a sledgehammer as a pincushion. Employed in 'penny packets' and in roles for which they were unsuited, its tanks were frittered away. In view of Pope's firm views about the use of armour, and the strength of his personality, it is difficult to believe that his presence and authority south of the Somme would not have brought more coherence and commonsense into those last and desperate days. Meanwhile, he did what he could in the crumbling theatre of the north. During the 23rd the Tank Brigade had again fought with great gallantry, under 'last man and last round' orders, and had preserved the flank of 5 and 50 Divisions on Vimy Ridge, but at an inevitable cost. When Pope visited the remnants next morning he found that the whole Brigade was now reduced to two of the gun-bearing Mk II Matildas and eighteen of the Mk I, *including* reserves. He therefore ordered a composite unit to be formed, and the 4th/7th Battalion (really a company) was created under Major Parkes who was to receive an immediate award of a DSO.

When he got back to GHQ he received a report from an officer who had been on a reconnaissance to Gravelines in an attempt to find out what was happening to 3 RTR in beleaguered Calais. He had discovered that Major Reeves with four tanks had broken out and was successfully holding Gravelines against German armoured assaults,* but that he was now short of ammunition. The entry in Pope's diary for the 24th begins characteristically: 'Decided to clear up situation at Gravelines and if possible Calais myself'. He therefore collected 96 rounds of 2-pounder ammunition and some machine-gun bullets from the 4th/7th and set off north to find Reeves. This he contrived to do, and after delivering his supplies and hearing the Major's adventures he was able to congratulate him and put him in for the immediate DSO which he was duly awarded. Then, 'with the aid of a very helpful and know-ledgeable signal officer,' he was able to get through to his old staff officer Liardet in the War Office in London, from whom he discovered that the remains of 3 RTR in Calais had been re-embarked, and there was nothing left for him to do.

Next morning he arranged at GHQ for the surplus officers and men of the Tank Brigade to be sent down to Dunkirk. It was suggested that he too should go home, but that was not to Pope's liking, and he sent Pratt instead. Then he went off to see to the composite company, and for the next 24 hours whirled about the bridgehead, unceasingly, supervising its activities. By the evening of the 27th there was no AFV work left for him to do. The 4th/7th was finished. Pownall, the Chief of Staff, ordered

* Reeves' account of his remarkable performance is on p. 20 in Vol. II of Liddell Hart, *The Tanks*.

him back to England, but Pope took evasive action and made his way down to La Panne, whence the evacuation was being conducted under General Adam. But Adam, like Pownall, had no job for Pope, and in view of the shortage of senior officers of the Royal Armoured Corps in England he was again, and finally, ordered to return. He was back in the War Office on the evening of the 28th.

CHAPTER TEN

NOW THRIVE THE ARMOURERS

'Noel asked me what kind of operations I was considering. I replied that I was considering war.'

Pope's *Diary*, 17 June, 1940

Before Pope allowed himself to be evacuated from Dunkirk he had taken a sensible precaution. When Brigadier Pratt returned on 26 May he carried with him a secret and personal letter addressed to Brigadier Kenchington at the War Office. Kenchington, who was later to command an armoured brigade at Alamein, was in those days Deputy Director of Staff Duties (AFV), and Pope had composed for him, as a precaution against being killed or captured in France, a summary of the main points he had learned 'as a result of bitter experience'. Someone, he felt, should let the guardians of the future have a few home truths.

The complete text of the letter is reproduced in Vol II of Liddell Hart's *The Tanks*. Its first and salient point was absolutely relevant to what had happened, but less so to the years ahead. 'There must', said Pope, 'be a *Commander* RAC in the Field with an adequate staff to enable him to command, and he must control all movements of all RAC troops as directed by the General Staff.' His own frustration at the lack of operational authority in France, and the inefficiency which flowed from it, have already been made plain. Formation commanders with infantry or cavalry attitudes had not been the best disposers of the few and precious tanks. But the ultimate answer did not lie here; it lay in the creation of armoured divisions whose commanders' recognized competence gave them a large authority in their own right, and the emergence of generals at the level of corps and army command who understood how to employ armour in the right way. Such, certainly, was the drift in the latter and victorious years of the war. A Commander RAC of the kind Pope pardonably envisaged was really a spare wheel.[*]

But his other points referred to needs of a pressing urgency: thicker armour on tanks, a gun for each and a better gun than the 2-pounder, mechanisms that would be simple and reliable, better armoured cars. '1st Army Tank Brigade', he recorded, 'walked through everything it met, but mechanical failures have wrecked it.' Uncertain whether he would ever see England again, he registered his faith. 'I do hope the Powers that be realize that the Boche has succeeded solely because of his mass of tanks supported by air attacks. Man for man we can beat him any day and twice a day....' Nigel Duncan, who was working in Whitehall at the time, commented:

'I remember this being read out in the War Office when we didn't think VV had a chance of getting back. However, he came back, through Dunkirk, still looking like death and working at a pace which astounded all those who didn't know him. That letter of his from France was a most far-reaching document. It put down, under the urgency of possible capture, all the things

[*] This is illustrated by the presence of Major-General McCreery as Adviser AFV at GHQ Middle East in the spring and summer of 1942. As *adviser* he was able to bring valuable pressure to bear on Auchinleck from the armoured viewpoint, but it is difficult to see how he could have effectively exercised *command* functions in the field. The nearest approach to Pope's ideal was Hitler's appointment of Guderian as Inspector General of Armoured Forces in the post-Stalingrad period.

that Vyvyan had held as essential when he was commanding 3rd Armd Bde and which had been confirmed by his experiences in action. No one believed it outside the Royal Armoured Corps, but if only attention had been paid to it, we should have been spared many casualties.'

Would attention be paid? In the Britain of 1940, living from hand to mouth, *could* attention be paid? These were the questions which preoccupied Pope continuously after his return to London. It was clear that he was marked for an important place in the mainstream of armoured policy, but in that mid-summer the waters were turbulent and muddy.

The organization for handling armour within the Ministry of Supply was not working smoothly and co-ordination with the Army was inadequate. There had already been public criticism, as a result of which there was appointed on 29 May, the day after Pope's return, a Tank Board charged 'to consider the whole situation regarding the production and design of tanks and to advise the Minister of Supply as to the future action'. How necessary this was may be gauged from the account in Pope's diary of his attendance on 5 June at a large meeting in the Ministry of Supply, summoned to discuss future armoured policy.

In the chair was Peter Bennett, Director-General of Tanks and Transport, and among those present were Major-General Lawrence Carr, 'the ACIGS with responsibility for tanks', Taylor, (the military adviser to the Ministry), and old friends like Kenchington and Pratt. Pope gave a long report on his experiences and made his recommendations. Most were agreed, but when he said that they must envisage within six to nine months a German output of more heavily armoured tanks and more effective anti-tank guns there was an uproar. (His intuition was, of course, right; nor had he appreciated that the German basic design was so sound that for long it was possible simply to improve, rather than to replace, the Marks III and IV.) 'These remarks caused a good deal of discussion, Peter Bennett maintaining that no new types of tank could be produced in under eighteen months. When I suggested mildly that the Germans seemed to work faster than we did, Bennett shouted excitedly that it was not so and that we should not get any new types earlier. Lawrence Carr asked him if that was the view of the Ministry and he said "Yes". Carr then dropped the subject, but I felt impelled to say that I was appalled to hear it, a remark that did not endear me to Bennett.' Nor was Pope himself appeased when, after he had stressed the need for reliability and simplicty of design, with a rejection of all frills, Taylor suggested that *wireless* was a frill.

'The whole atmosphere was one of obstinate defeatism. "We have done all that men can do, and more. Why will you ask us for the impossible? You must trust the men who gave you the faulty A12 transmission and the A13 skidding track, and who are rectifying these mistakes only a few months after you had drawn their attention to them. After all, we are experts and we know; you are only the poor fools who have to fight the tanks we provide, mere cannon-fodder. Why do you fuss us so and try to disturb our programmes?" It is perfectly clear to me that while this gang remain in control, nothing effective will be done.'

But at least the control was now to be changed. The Tank Board acted with commendable speed. Its recommendations were produced on 7 June, and on the 11th the Minister of Supply announced in the Commons that he and the War Minister had accepted them. In future, military officers in the Ministry of Supply would be replaced by expert civilians, and an officer of high rank with recent experience of tank fighting would be appointed to represent the requirements of the Army to the Ministry. 'The Army', the Board had observed, 'must state its demands unequivocally and through one focal point'. Within a fortnight Major-General Vyvyan Pope had been appointed to the new post of Director of Armoured Fighting Vehicles, to become that necessary focus.

Before he took up his post, however, Pope had to appear before another committee which, under General Bartholomew, was reviewing the lessons to be learned from the French campaign, a committee, Pope mordantly observed, which was indicative of British attitudes towards armour, since it consisted of three infantrymen and two gunners examining a battle which had been won by the action of air and armoured forces. When he presented himself, on the 17th, he found among the interrogators his Staff College contemporary Noel Irwin, whom he had recently assisted in France when Irwin for a time commanded 2 Division.

'Noel Irwin began by asking me what was the smallest number of tanks I would consider decentralizing under command of another formation. I replied "an Armoured Division". Noel asked me what kind of operation I was considering. I replied that I was considering war, and that the principles of war remained the same whether we were fighting in France or in England. There was then a good deal of wrangling from which I gathered that the Committee was abandoning its task of studying the lessons learned and devoting itself to the task of the defence of England, and that Noel Irwin in particular was anxious to form penny packets of brigade groups containing all arms and tanks and to scatter them broadcast. I made it very clear that I could not subscribe to any doctrine of that kind, that our experience had shown that distribution of armoured forces led to defeat in detail since it was not possible to ensure that adequate numbers could be placed in the right place at the right time, and that in defence armoured troops should be held concentrated in reserve ready to strike when required.'

This was the correct and classic doctrine, which Alan Brooke as C-in-C Home Forces did in fact apply in his preparations to meet a German invasion. That there was a division of opinion among the Germans on this point, when they too had to meet an invasion, is not relevant, since by 1944 a new factor had entered the equation—the domination of road and rail communications by Allied air-power. So while von Rundstedt and Geyr von Schweppenburg had good reason for following the classic prescription and holding their armour *en masse* and well inland, Rommel also had a case for arguing that it should be distributed in small units much nearer the sea. But in 1940 the Luftwaffe, though strong, was not capable of interrupting movement in Britain, and in the face of the RAF, to anything like the same extent. Thus Pope's affirmation before the Bartholomew Committee was unquestionably the right one, as appropriate to the British situation in mid-summer, 1940, as it would prove to be when he reached Africa in September, 1941.

The new Major-General was at a pivotal point of great influence and responsibility. His drive, experience and high standards, together with the great respect he commanded, seemed just what was required during that period of Britain's nakedness to vitalize the force of armour which must now be brought into being if the island was to be defended and counter-offensives undertaken in due course. But a realistic eye perceives that though there was much he could and did do there was much that lay beyond his grasp. He was the inheritor of years of folly. Governments, General Staffs and the civil service had between them so mishandled procedures for the design and production of tanks that the world Pope now entered was less an efficient organization than chaos. The ill-conceived systems of the 'thirties, the failure to hand on to the men of the 'forties clear principles of sound design and well-tested methods of construction, (the opposite of what happened in Germany) had the ignominious result that Britain's armoured divisions were only saved from disaster by the arrival of an American tank, the Sherman, in 1942. Thus Pope was more concerned with putting things right and keeping things going than with introducing original and creative ideas. He could add leaven to the lump, but the lump was inescapable.

His second limiting factor was that Britain, having survived an evacuation, now faced an invasion without the arms which had been lost in France. The equipment available in the country on the morrow of Dunkirk was not enough to supply more than two divisions, and there remained less than 100 tanks—of all ages and descriptions. The emphasis, under Churchill's inevitable insistence, was on quantity and the immediately available. During the whole period of Pope's service as DAFV, from June, 1940, to September, 1941, it is fair to say that novelties and improvements were at a discount. The policy was that of the bird in the hand.

Two instances will suffice. Pope saw clearly that the Germans would up-gun and increasingly protect with armour the Panzers of the *Blitzkrieg*—as they did. He required a 6-pounder gun—forecasting its necessity while still in France and arguing for it on his return. But the combination of those who 'knew better' and immediate urgencies defeated him; the claim that to bring the

6-pounder into production would interrupt the existing flow of weapons was unanswerable. In consequence the first few 6-pounder anti-tank guns were not in action until Gazala in the summer of 1942, though their quality was to be revealed from Alamein onwards. And for month after weary month the tank crews in the desert fought the *Afrika Korps* with 2-pounders, which, however much the experts might argue, had no great reputation with those whose lives depended on them.

Again, among Pope's recommendations on his return was one for 'a super-heavy tank designed for position warfare', by which he meant a large, powerful infantry tank, capable of working in rough ground, with an anti-tank gun larger than a 2-pounder. At a meeting of the Tank Board on 11 June the Prime Minister quite independently ordered a crash programme to produce 5–600 of the A22, (later named the 'Churchill'), which in many ways came to fit in with Pope's prescription. The first production models were emerging within a year, an astonishing achievement in the circumstances. But this programme, imposed on the existing flow of obsolescent tanks which were being produced simply because they could be produced, made the introduction of new and up-to-date designs even more unlikely. Moreover, gambling on what might be made quickly available proved a mistake, for the Churchills, which went more or less straight from the drawing-board into production, developed many snags, and even by 1942 there were still defects awaiting elimination. For these and other reasons, therefore, Pope in his work as Director was tied to the unavoidable rather than free to explore the desirable.

Except in one respect. By the end of 1940 four armoured divisions—1, 6, 8 and 9—were in existence,* and a fifth, 11,

* As well as 7 Armoured Division in North Africa and 2 Armoured Division in transit thither.

was raised early in the next year. Pope was not only concerned with the equipment of these and future formations; they had to be manned. A vast new empire of training regiments, specialist schools, officer cadet units and so on was therefore progressively developed to produce the thousands of soldiers, tank commanders and staff required for these new divisions—new in every sense, for, as has been seen, British policy between the wars had denied the Army the opportunity of acquiring much experience in this complex and difficult role. All this immense expansion fell within Pope's ambit, and here, at least, it was possible to create and construct. The standards of skill and efficiency attained by the enormous armoured forces Britain finally acquired owed much to the foundations laid in the training establishments during Pope's period as DAFV. Nigel Duncan served under him as the G 1 staff officer with special responsibility for this work:

'Vyvyan came round to see training in progress at both regiments and OCTUs and after that gave me a completely free hand. I used to report to him weekly to tell him what was on and I had immediate access if I was in difficulties. He was an ideal man to serve from that angle—once he trusted you you were left in peace to work out your own salvation under a broad charter which defined the requirements and left you to produce them. It was always fun working for him and he was always very appreciative of any special effort made for him. What never ceased to astound me was the completeness of his grasp of all the details that were affecting the RAC at the time. It was easy for us on his staff— we were closely concerned with all this but he knew it as well as we did, but it never affected his grasp of the wider issues. It was very rarely necessary to brief him in detail before a conference—he had it at his finger-tips.

131

We saw him go with great regret; it was obvious that he must, he was far too good to keep out of the field. Before he went he had put the RAC Directorate, as it later became, on the firmest foundations; he supplied the drive, he demanded the performance and the standards out of everyone under him and he commanded un-limited respect and affection from all who came into contact with him.

Much of this is implied in a single entry in Alan Brooke's diary for 18 September. 'Spent the day in the office with a series of interviews. First Pope to settle the future of Armoured Corps. . . .'

If, that same autumn, a Lance-Corporal in the Home Guard at Chipping Camden had responded differently to the overtures of his Prime Minister, Pope might well have obtained a powerful ally. It was to this obscurity that Hobart had withdrawn when, in March and incon-ceivably, he was put on retired pay. In August, however, Liddell Hart published an article in the *Sunday Pictorial* entitled 'We Have Wasted Brains', in which he pointed out that none of the generals who knew most about armour, Fuller, Lindsay, Pile, Martel and Hobart, were now com-manding tanks. Interest in Hobart revived. He was first offered a Ministry of Supply job in connection with tank production, but wrote, 'I can't see there's room for anyone but Pope in that line, and I don't want to jockey him.' Then, through Pile, Churchill's attention was focused on Hobart just when the Prime Minister was feeling for some-one to put in overall control of Britain's armour. When he was offered the job Hobart's demands proved too sweeping for the War Office—a seat on the Army Council and virtually plenary powers—but he was given the new 11 Armoured Division and embarked on that brilliant new career which, in the latter stages of the war, found him commanding on the Continent a larger armoured force than has ever been under the direct control of a British officer. It is impossible, however, not to speculate on the possible fruits of a marriage between this wayward genius and his more stable and balanced friend. Hobart in full control, with Pope as his lieutenant, would have been a formidable combination: Pope's operational and administrative experience, and Hobart's creative fire.

In the event a smaller man got a smaller job. It was Martel who, in January, 1941, was appointed to the new post of Commander RAC, 'charged with the development of armoured technique and the preparation for battle of armoured formations.' But this was not the overlordship Hobart had sought. Martel had a split responsibility—to the CIGS and to C-in-C Home Forces. He had no seat on the Army Council. He was specifically excluded from the design and output of tanks, which continued to fall within Pope's sphere. So did the training establishments and schools. Recruits were processed under Pope and handed over to Martel when they passed out. 'General Pope and myself naturally had to work very closely together,' Martel wrote in his memoirs, *An Outspoken Soldier*, 'and we did so very easily and pleasantly.'

So he may have thought. Martel, however, was a man who wore rose-tinted spectacles. His technical contributions to the development of British armour were considerable from its earliest days, but his invincible self-complacency, which pervades his autobiography, made him exaggerate his own importance, understate that of others, and act stupidly because he was blissfully unaware that his folly was obvious. All those who observed Pope at this time agree that he took Martel with a pinch of salt. They were not men of the same dimensions. If there was no explosion, it was probably because, in the ill-defined area for which Martel had been given responsibility, the boundaries of Pope's own territory had been very clearly demarcated.

As the spring of 1941 ran on, and disasters in the Balkans accompanied defeat in North Africa by the newly arrived Rommel, concern about the quantity and quality of British tank production was widespread. A minute followed.

Prime Minister to Secretary of State for War and Minister of Supply.   24 Apr 41

I propose to hold periodical meetings to consider tank and anti-tank questions, the first of which will be at 10 Downing Street on Monday, 5 May, at 11 am. These meetings would be attended by yourselves, accompanied by appropriate officers. From the War Office I would propose that the CIGS, ACIGS, and General Pope should come, and General Martel and his Armoured Divisional Commanders should also be invited. . . .

2. I am particularly anxious that all officers attending the meeting should be encouraged to send their suggestions as to the points which should be discussed, and to express their individual views with complete freedom, I contemplate, in fact, a 'Tank Parliament'.

Martel, however, set out to sabotage this promising project. What was necessary at this stage of the war was a powerful and properly guided impulsion from the top, and the Tank Parliament (which never prospered) might have been shaped into a valuable instrument for this purpose. But Martel describes with glee in his autobiography how he would assemble his divisional commanders beforehand, discuss the probable issues which would arise, and concert the answers which they would unanimously offer. (Hobart refused to play.) This nullified Churchill's declared desire for free and open discussion. Of course

Martel's tactics were observed by the Prime Minister and no doubt contributed to his ultimate disappearance from the scene. But the relevant point is that such childish manoeuvres in matters of the highest concern were anathema to a man like Pope, sophisticated, serious, and intimately aware of the situation's urgency. He was not, of course, under Martel's orders at the Parliament, but came from the War Office: otherwise there might well have been a showdown.*

The urgency of the situation was sharply reflected in an American's diary. General Raymond E. Lee was technically the military attaché at the US Embassy in London; in practice his function was to keep the Pentagon and the President supplied with up-to-date and on-the-spot estimates as to Britain's capacity to survive. On 5 May he gave a dinner to Pope and Martel in his room at Claridge's.

> 'What I wanted from these people was a frank exposition of the serious situation in tanks so that I could reinforce a cable which I had had drafted for some days, requesting and urging the despatch of a tank mission over here who will get first a sense of the urgency of the question and second will form the foundation of a joint board on making tanks and standardizing design.'†

Next day he followed this up by calling on Pope at the War Office:

> 'They finally gave me a complete resumé of the tank

---

* Martel did, in fact, pay a generous tribute to Pope, writing that 'it was his work as DAFV at the War Office for which he will always be remembered by the Corps. The organization of the Armoured Division in its present form (1941) is mainly his work.'

† *The London Observer: The Journal of General Raymond E. Lee*, p. 267. (Hutchinson, 1972).

situation and I must say that it is a very discouraging picture. What they need now is about 1,500 tanks straight away. I don't see where they are going to come from.'

Pope's estimate was underlined by the fact that at that very moment Churchill's great *coup*, the TIGER convoy, was about to deliver in Egypt the precious tanks which had been rushed straight through the Mediterranean as a counter to the new threat from the *Afrika Korps*. 295 tanks had left Britain and all but 57 arrived, including the latest Crusader cruisers. This consignment, on which Churchill had built such high hopes, intimately affected Pope's destiny.

The sequence is direct. Reinforced by the 'Tiger cubs', Wavell reluctantly launched his BATTLEAXE offensive in mid-June, and was comprehensively defeated. Churchill then removed Wavell, in a final fit of exasperation, and replaced him with Auchinleck, who stubbornly refused to undertake a new offensive until his newly-named 8th Army was ready. At last the pressure became irresistible, and plans began to be laid for a major new offensive in the desert, called CRUSADER. The Army would comprise two Corps: 13, consisting of infantry, and 30, the armoured Corps, whose function would be to find and destroy the Panzers. Pope was given 30 Corps.

The notion that Auchinleck was 'a bad picker' and inclined to favour his beloved Indian Army can only be partly substantiated. That some of his choices were ill-judged cannot be questioned. But in setting up the higher command of CRUSADER his approach is documented and unimpeachable. On 16 August he wrote to the CIGS, Sir John Dill: 'I realize very well that I am taking a risk in removing commanders who have fought in the Desert, and that my suggested replacements are new to that part of the world. In spite of this drawback I think the changes should be carried out. I feel in my bones that the windows and doors need opening very wide so that fresh air and new ideas can enter, and I believe that this would more than offset any initial and temporary lack of local knowledge in the new man.' Lieutenant-General Sir Arthur Smith, then Auchinleck's Chief of Staff, has confirmed to the author that his master's only concern was to get for CRUSADER the best men he could. Apart from Sir Alan Cunningham, who now took command of 8th Army after his victories in East Africa, the key appointment was obviously that of Pope, since 30 Corps was envisaged as the hammer with which the Panzers would be shattered and Tobruk relieved. Nor did he suffer from an 'initial and temporary lack of local knowledge'. He already had sand in his shoes.

Anyone who flew with Wavell during the war offered hostages to fortune; he seemed to cast an evil eye on aircraft, which habitually misbehaved under his burden all over the world. For the first part of his journey to Africa Pope was free of this threat, for he travelled out to Gibraltar in a Catalina with Liardet, who was to be on his staff, and though their pilot lost his way over the Atlantic they recovered course and landed safely on the morning of 21 September. That evening, they were joined at Government House by Arthur Smith and Wavell, *en route* from London for India where he was now Commander-in-Chief. After an overnight stay with Lord Gort, the Governor, they were due to depart in their flying-boat about midday. The passengers consisted of Wavell, Pope, Smith, two RAF officers and Wavell's ADC. Jonah was obviously aboard, for a wind got up and after three attempts to take off the Catalina crashed into a large wave, which tore open the floor of the forward cabin and let the ocean in.

'The sequence', Pope wrote in what was his last diary entry, 'was bump—bump—crash—smash followed by the instantaneous shutting off of the engines and a simultaneous spurt of water through the bottom of the boat into the cabin. There were cries of "get out", "shut the bulkheads", and a scurrying of the crew hither and thither, as jets of bright green water shot up through the floorboards. I released my grip of the bunk to which I had been clinging like a monkey and seized my dispatch case, British warm and Sam Browne but left my hat behind. When I got into the gunner's compartment an airman from the top of the compartment exhorted me to climb on the roof as being safer. I did so with some difficulty.' (It is always easy to forget that Pope had no right arm.) Arthur Smith was impressed by the oddity of their appearance; Wavell with only one eye, Pope with only one arm, the ADC also with only one eye and Smith himself with only one and a half legs.

A launch then arrived to tow the Catalina to a slipway, but the damage was done and it was not Wavell's day. John Connell, his biographer, records one of his more intimate embarrassments:[*] 'The newspapers were a soggy mess; much of the Chief's kit was badly spoiled by sea water and fuel oil; one very damp brown paper parcel was opened to reveal a brassière—a present for one of the girls[†] put into Wavell's baggage at the last minute by his sisters; and all his secret papers had had a dunking.' Thereafter, however, all went safely if slowly, and after some delay in Malta they finally reached Cairo on 25 September.

Liddell Hart made a slip in *The Tanks* when he wrote of Pope's death that he 'had already made his mark as Major-General AFV at GHQ Middle East, and was about

[*] John Connell, *Wavell, Supreme Commander*, p. 32.
[†] Not 'les girls', but his daughters!

to take command of an armoured corps in the field'. He was MGAFV Middle East from 20 to 24 September only,* and clearly went into full gear as soon as he reached Cairo, where he had been immediately promoted to Lieutenant-General, on taking command of his Corps. This was imperative, for CRUSADER loomed, there was much to be done, and he was a Corps Commander without a headquarters. Within a few days, however, he had gathered a staff,† and on 5 October he set off 'up the desert' to attend General Cunningham's first 8th Army conference on the battle.

He took with him his BGS, Brigadier Hugh Russell, his AQMG, Brigadier Eric Unwin, and his ADC, Captain G. R. Amery. His AAQMG, (now Major-General Liardet), stayed behind—and saved his life. Their Hudson got into difficulties on take-off, crashed into the Mocattam Hills, and all aboard were killed. One possibility seemed to be that an engine had cut out and the pilot had made a split-second error in banking the wrong way.

Twenty years before, after hearing at the Queen's Hall a performance of Holst's setting of Whitman's *Ode to Death*, Pope had entered in his notebooks some reflections —among which was the feeling that the *Ode* was too consolatory. But then he wrote down some lines from the *Ode* of which he entirely approved:

> 'Death who reapest with an equal hand, deaf to
> our cries, blind to our misery,
> The priest and the sacrifice, the judge and the
> condemned,
> The statesman and the assassin,
> Whose stroke is sure and unflinching,
> Death the unchanging change, thee I salute.'

* Presumably to keep up his pay during the journey.
† The headquarters of his new Corps (called, temporarily, K Corps—it became 30 Corps on 21 October) was formally established on 2 October.

CHAPTER ELEVEN

CRUSADER: A POSTSCRIPT

'Our experience had shown that distribution of armoured
forces led to defeat in detail.'

Vyvyan Pope, June, 1940

'Fighting in detail, the Celts were conquered wholesale.'

Tacitus

The British offensive in the desert opened on 18 November, 1941, but Lieutenant-General Vyvyan Pope, CBE, DSO, MC was 'left'—in the old army phrase—'out of battle'. The funeral with its military honours had taken place; a firing party from the Royal Tank Regiment had made the last salute with their revolvers; his successor had been appointed. Pope was already part of the past.

But though the historian is rigorously concerned with what happened rather than with what might have been, the biographer has a different interest and responsibility. It is but common justice to one's subject to ask whether the future of the British in North Africa would have been different, and different for the better, if chance had not carried that crippled Hudson onto the Mocattam Hills. Analysts still consider, from time to time, what would have been the fortune of 8th Army in the following year if Gott's plane had not been shot down as he was flying to take over its command; if, in fact, he had not been replaced by Montgomery. Yet 'Strafer' Gott, unfortunate as Pope in his way of death, was luckier in life, for his reputation had already been established on the battlefield. As Pope stepped into the aircraft at Heliopolis he was approaching the apex of his military career. Years of thought and training were now to be brought to bear on the task which, for every true soldier, is the greatest—a high command in a critical battle. That he would have acquitted himself well is certain. That he might have done more, and thereby made for himself a memorable name, is not beyond possibility. But the plane crashed, and the war went on. For him, in Rommel's words, there were 'No laurels in Africa'.

The effect Pope might have had on CRUSADER may best be deduced from the actual course of the battle, which undoubtedly owed much to the character and experience of the man who replaced him. Willoughby Norrie was on his way from England when Pope died, moving in advance of the ships transporting his 1st Armoured Division. He was available, he was fresh, he was possible, and he was given the job. But it is no disrespect to an old Hussar of great gallantry to say that in understanding and experience of armour he fell short of his predecessor. Pope's contemporary at the Staff College, he had served with exceptional distinction in the Tank Corps during the First World War, winning as a young officer the DSO and MC and bar, and being wounded four times. Between the wars, however, he had spent from 1926 to 1938 commanding the 10th Hussars and as Brigade Major and, finally, commander of 1st Cavalry Brigade. These twelve years were not the best background for tackling, in 1941, the Panzers of an *Afrika Korps* with two victories already to its credit. Moreover, through no fault of his own he had not time to build up a new and smooth-running headquarters or to get to know his Corps—still less the desert—before the offensive was launched. On several counts, therefore, it is not surprising if the British armour's performance in CRUSADER, superb though it often was at the unit and individual level, is marked throughout by a lack of firm control at the top.

Many would maintain that CRUSADER was nearly lost in the first twenty-four hours, and that the British were only saved from the consequences of their initial errors by Rommel himself, whose notorious 'dash to the wire' in the middle of the battle allowed his opponents time to draw breath and reorganize. Such critics point to Cunningham's opening gambit. With his infantry Corps, 13, he pushed against the Italians facing him in the north, while his armoured Corps, 30, was ordered to advance to the general area of Gabr Saleh, some fifty miles south-east of Tobruk, and halt there to await Rommel's response—the hope being that he would come forward in strength, a great tank battle would follow and the victorious British would then sweep on to the relief of Tobruk. But nothing happened—except that the initiative had been handed to Rommel. 'Cunningham had travelled with Norrie in order to keep closely in touch with the situation and be able to make the great decision, on reaching Gabr Saleh, as to what to do next, based on the reactions of the enemy. The trouble was that there did not seem to be any enemy, and certainly no recognizable reaction. It was perhaps a pity for his purpose that the elaborate measures to achieve surprise had been so successful. No firm decision for action was therefore made.'*

Nor could the decisions that were finally taken be called firm, for, during the next two days, they led to such dispositions that von Mellenthin, then on Rommel's staff, was to write: 'Cunningham had been obliging enough to scatter 7 Armoured Division all over the desert'. 22 Armoured Brigade was directed on Bir Gubi, due south of Tobruk, where its raw Yeomanry regiments, disregarding the advice of the desert-wise 11th Hussars, attacked a

* Michael Carver, *Tobruk*, p. 48.

fortified strongpoint held by the excellent Italian *Ariete* Division and lost half their strength. Away to the north 7 Armoured Brigade occupied Sidi Rezegh airfield, the threshold of Tobruk. But at the same time 4 Armoured Brigade was still back near Gabr Saleh, protecting the southern flank of 13 Corps and even sending some of its armoured cars and tanks *north-east* in a dash towards the sea. After the battle Rommel said to a captured senior officer: 'What difference does it make if you have two tanks to my one, when you spread them out and let me smash them in detail? You presented me with three brigades in succession.'

Though the outcome of this long and terrible conflict was a transient victory for 8th Army—after cruel losses and the sacking of Cunningham—the possibility of imposing a clean-cut pattern on the battle was thrown away by this opening scatter of the armour. As the flower of the British tank crews were destroyed piecemeal it ceased to be possible to re-unite into larger formations or, when a relaxing of German pressure did make it worth trying, to group together enough of the surviving tanks to make a dominant force. Most of CRUSADER was hectic, scurried, improvised, desperate. Auchinleck's will and the courage of individuals triumphed in the end, but what Pope had stated in 1940 still applied: 'Our experience had shown that distribution of armoured forces led to defeat in detail.' Moreover, the victory was far less than decisive. Rommel was compelled to retreat, but when he had gathered strength for a counter-attack 8th Army lacked the power to resist, and itself was driven back to what, a few months later, would prove to be the fatal line of Gazala.

Against this bitter-sweet record Pope's declared views stand out in firm and simple outline. One remembers his testimony before the Bartholomew Committee just after Dunkirk. 'The principles of war remained the same whether we were fighting in France or in England'—no broadcast scattering of armoured brigade groups. Concentrate, concentrate. Raymond Briggs remembered how scornful he was of the 'Jock columns' which were modish in the desert. Liardet, one of the last to see him alive, recalled how 'V.V.P. several times said to me that our biggest mistake in France and in the desert was to 'penny packet' our armour. He said to me, "That is one thing I will never do. *I will keep and fight the armour concentrated whatever happens."* ' Could he, had he lived, have managed to fight 30 Corps *en masse*?

If Pope had survived to become CIGS, as acute observers thought he might, he would have been the first member of the Royal Tank Regiment to do so. That distinction was reserved for Field-Marshal Sir Michael Carver, who discusses this question in his *Tobruk* with the authority of one who is an 'old desert hand' and who has subsequently studied with a historian's eye the campaigns in which he fought. In his view, 'It would have needed a commander of great clarity of thought, wide experience not only of tank training, but also of tactics generally, and also the authority to impose unpopular decisions and concepts, to have discerned the real needs of the moment, organized the revolution in thought and practice needed and given effect to it on the battlefield. It is possible, though unlikely, that Vyvyan Pope might have done all this; but with his death, before he led his Corps into battle, there was no other with the necessary combination of qualities.'

From that carefully weighted judgement it is difficult to make an appeal, other than to observe that in drawing it up there was not available to the Field-Marshal the fuller picture of Pope's attitudes, experience and personality which these pages provide. Yet it is precisely the knowledge of what he was and thought which suggests possibilities greater than Sir Michael was prepared to accept when he published *Tobruk* in 1964. In the opening phase of CRUSADER two major errors occurred. Cunningham, as has been seen, allowed his armour to scatter. Norrie would have preferred to hold it together and drive straight for Sidi Rezegh, but he capitulated to his Army Commander. The extra fast brigade, 4 Armoured, was pinned back in an uneasy protective role on the left flank of 13 Corps, instead of being combined with the two other armoured brigades in 30 Corps, because the infantry commanders in 13 Corps were afraid of Panzer attacks and clamoured insistently for more support—though they already had the 132 Valentines and Matildas of 1 Army Tank Brigade under command. On this point, too, Norrie was uneasy, wishing to retain 4 Armoured in its proper role as part of the striking force: but again Cunningham over-ruled him—with painful results. From these two false premises the logic of CRUSADER inevitably flowed. Would Pope have made a difference?

The central problem was a crisis of authority. The stated object of CRUSADER, laid down by Auchinleck, was to smash the Panzers of the *Afrika Korps*: all else was subsidiary because all other desirable consequences would follow such a success. What was required, therefore, was a clear and simple scheme designed for that main purpose and evidently likely to achieve it, employing available resources at the key point and including nothing vague or contingent; intelligible to all and imposed on all, whether they like it or not. (One is insensibly drawn into describing a Montgomery battle-plan.) Cunningham failed to produce such a scheme, but then Cunningham, above all, lacked the necessary authority or self-confidence. CRUSADER was to be essentially an armoured battle and he knew nothing relevant about armour. What he needed at his side, therefore, was an armoured commander with clarity of vision, experience, manifest authority and a strong will, whose judgement he respected and whose ideas about fighting the battle he was prepared to accept as overriding, in view of his own lack of expertise in this special field. Norrie failed to achieve such an ascendancy and the result was not only an unsophisticated plan for the armour but also a readiness to let the natural self-interest of the infantry Corps weaken the main battle-plan.

Pope had authority. He had arrived from England as the War Office choice in response to Auchinleck's specific request.* Norrie, by contrast, and through no fault of his own, was a last-minute stop-gap. Pope came with a long record of diverse experience in armour. Norrie had neither the equivalent technical equipment nor the habit of working at the highest level of affairs. Above all, the record of Pope's life shows that he had a spirit of tempered steel combined with intellectual qualities of unusual range and depth. He was not given to compromise with the incorrect or the second-rate. Taking Sir Michael Carver's doubts into account, therefore, it still seems possible to calculate that Pope might have been able to come to terms with Cunningham, might have been able to insist on a more coherent battle-plan, and by keeping his armour concentrated might have won a decisive instead of a dubious victory. And if that had happened, if Rommel had truly been hurled back in rout, who can tell what the consequences might have been? One thing is certain. Pope would no longer have been a footnote in history.

Unfortunately a commander in the end is dependent on the tools at his disposal. The strength and the fighting skill of 8th Army in November, 1941, were less impressive in fact than they appeared to be on paper. Over 700 tanks,

* In a letter to Mrs Pope after his death the CIGS, Sir John Dill, said that the War Office had wished to retain him but had had to admit reluctantly that he was the right man for the job.

compared with Rommel's 174 Mk III and Mk IV in the *Afrika Korps* and 146 'tin cans', the Italian M13s, seems a substantial majority. But the 158 Crusaders of 22 Armoured Brigade were new and unreliable, and the three Yeomanry regiments in the Brigade were fresh arrivals, untrained in the desert. 7 Armoured Brigade had a miscellany of cruisers of which too many were obsolescent or out-of-date. The American 'Honeys' of 4 Armoured Brigade were fast but light, and limited in range. The 132 infantry tanks with 13 Corps played no part in the main battle. On the other hand the Germans, now well supplied with the long 50 mm anti-tank gun and a useful number of 88 mm, were massively superior in this critical arm. But there was a deeper flaw. The tactics of tank fighting had still not been sufficiently mastered by the British. Infantry, armour and artillery—and air forces—had still to learn the techniques of fighting in unison.

Still, CRUSADER *was* a victory—a victory because Rommel had been pushed off the ground by sustained determination and the simple quality of courage. His own errors made their important contribution, but the *Afrika Korps* had matched its enemies in ardour. The unresolved question therefore remains: suppose 8th Army, in spite of its limitations of skill and equipment, had been able to exhibit the same tenacity and spirit in furtherance of a better plan, what might the consequences have been? Would Rommel have fallen back for ever, and Hitler have lost interest in North Africa? Might Auchinleck have survived, and Montgomery lost his chance? Could the character of the war in the Mediterranean have been radically altered? Certainly it is difficult not to believe that, just as Gott's plane-crash improved the prospects for Alamein, so Pope's diminished those for CRUSADER. Implicit in that thought is the meaning and the magnitude of his loss.

INDEX

Cambrai, 23, 45, 52, 69n, 106, 114
Canal Brigade (1936), 85, 93
Carr, Major-Gen Lawrence, 125–6
Carver, Field-Marshal Sir Michael, 142n, 144–6
Caunter, Col 'Blood', 88
Charteris, Gen John, 16
Chindits, the, 75
'Christmas truce' (1914), 11–13
Churchill, (Sir) Winston, 28, 63, 77, 119, 129, 130, 132, 134–6
Churchill tank, 130
Clarke, Brig Dudley, 86
Collins, Michael, 47
Connell, John, 99n, 138 and n
Cork, 48–51; Lord Mayor of, 45; Infantry Regiment, 48
Covenanter tank, 107
Crusader tank, 95, 107, 136, 147
Cunningham, Gen Sir Alan, 137, 139, 142, 143, 145, 146
Curragh, the, 41; Mutiny (1914), 5; Brigade (1920), 42

Delville Wood, 19
Dempsey, Lieut-Gen Sir Miles, 111 and n
Denikin, Gen, 30
Desert Rats, 53, 56
  see also Armoured Division, 7th
Dill, Field-Marshal Sir John, 104, 136, 146n
Dublin, 42, 44–6, 48, 50, 51; Command, 47
Duncan, Major-Gen Nigel, 2, 68–9, 72–5, 85, 106–7, 124–5, 131–3
Dunkirk, evacuation from, 3, 101, 102n, 108, 121–3, 129, 143
Dunphie, Col Peter, 97

East Riding Yeomanry, 108, 113
East Surrey Regiment, 18
Economia island, 39, 40
Egypt, 51–7
Eighth Army, 1, 2, 54, 86n, 136, 137, 140, 143, 146, 147; 13 Corps, 136, 142, 143, 145–7; 30 Corps, 136, 137, 139 and n, 142, 144, 145
  see also Armoured Brigades and Armoured Divisions

8th Hussars, 86
11th Hussars, 84, 86, 88, 142
Escaut bridges, 112–13
Evans, Major-Gen, 118–20
Experimental Mechanized Force (1928), 70, 71, 85, 100

Fife and Forfar Yeomanry, 108
5th Division (1940), 111
5th Inniskillings, 108
15th/10th Hussars, 108
50th Infantry Division, 115, 116
51st Highland Division, 15n
Finch, Major-Gen Lionel, 65–6
First Army Corps (1 Corps) (1939–1940), 103, 104, 111, 112
1st Army Tank Brigade (1940), 108, 109, 111, 112, 114, 115, 120, 121, 124, 145
1st Cavalry Brigade, 141
1st Light Armoured Reconnaissance Brigade, 108
Foundations of a Science of War, The (Fuller), 76
4th/7th Dragoons, 108
Franklyn, Major-Gen, 114–16, 118
Freikorps, 28
French Cavalry Corps (1940), 114, 116
Friend, Brig, 84
Fuller, Major-Gen, J. F. C., 57, 61, 62, 68n, 69, 70, 76, 132

Gabe, Saleh, 142, 143
Gamelin, Gen, 103, 105
Gazala line (1942), 130, 143
Generals and Generalship (Wavell), 101
Georges, Gen, 120
German tanks, 125–6, 147
Godwin-Austen, Lieut-Gen, 61, 63
Gort, Field-Marshal Viscount, 3, 75, 102, 104, 107, 108, 118, 120, 137
Gott, Lieut-Gen W. H. E. ('Strafer'), 140, 148
Gough, Gen Sir Hubert, 16
Grand Quartier Général (GQC), 120
Grant tank, 71
Gravelines, 121

149

Graves, Robert, 8
Guards Armoured Division, 4
Guderian, Gen, 3, 57, 78, 79, 124n

Haig, Field-Marshal Earl, 16, 62, 75n
Hamilton, Gen Sir Ian, 5
Harper, 'Uncle', 15 and n
Hazebrouck, 118
Hitler, 79, 86, 90, 94, 99, 104–5, 115, 124n, 147
Hoare, Sir Samuel, 82
Hobart, Major-Gen Sir Percy, 3–5, 53, 62, 72, 74, 75, 90, 107, 132–134; commands Tank Brigade, 80–5, 87–9
Holst, Gustav, 139
Hood, HMS, 82
Hore-Belisha, Leslie, 98
Horrocks, Lieut-Gen Sir Brian, 3
Hulluch, 20
Huxley, Aldous, 5

Imperial Defence College, 80
Infantry in tracked and armoured vehicles, 71
Iraq, RAF in, 53
IRA (Irish Republican Army), 41, 42, 47, 50
Irish Agricultural Board, 44
Irish Treaty (1921), 49, 51
Irish troubles (1920–2), 42–51
Ironside, Field-Marshal Lord, 32–33, 38, 61, 75–6
Irwin, Gen Sir Noel, 61, 123, 127
Italy and Abyssinia, 82–4, 90, 94

Kenchington, Brig, 74, 123, 125
King-Hall, Sir Stephen, 63
Kitchener of Khartoum, Field-Marshal Earl, 14
Kolchak, Admiral, 30

Laird, Brig Kenneth, 74
Langdale, Sir Marmaduke, 1
La Panne, 122
Lawrence, T. E., 38, 52, 60; quoted, 28
Lee, Gen Raymond E., 135–6
Leese, Gen Sir Oliver, 116, 118
Leinster Regiment, 13

Lens, 115, 116
L'Epinette, capture of, 14
Liardet, Major-Gen H. M., 84–5, 121, 137, 139, 144
Liddell, Hart, Sir Basil, 57, 59 and n, 61n, 69–71, 76n, 78, 80, 86, 87n, 88–9, 93–4, 121n, 123, 132, 138–9
Lindsay, George, 3, 57, 69, 72, 87, 90, 132
Lindsell, Gen Sir Wilfrid, 1, 61'
Long Range Desert Group, 57
Loos, battle of (1915), 16
Luftwaffe, 100, 128

McCreery, Gen Sir Richard, 86n, 124n
Machine Gun Corps, 54
Mareth Line, 3, 54
Marshall, Gen George C., 2
Martel, Gen Sir Giffard, 62, 69, 116, 117, 132–5; Commander, RAC, 133–5
Matilda tank, 96, 115, 117, 120, 145
Mechanized and Armoured Formations (the 'Purple Primer'), 77–9
Mellenthin, von, 142
Mersa Matruh, Mobile Force at (1936), 70, 84, 89
Messines, battle of (1917), 21
Milne, Field-Marshal Sir George (Lord Milne), 61, 69, 76
Ministry of Supply, 125–7, 132
Mitford, Brig, 20
Mobile Division (1938), 96
Mobile Force for defence of Egypt (1936), 70, 82–90, 94, 95
Montgomery of Alamein, Field-Marshal Visct, 1, 7, 48, 51, 100, 102, 140, 145, 148
Montgomery-Massingberd, Field-Marshal Sir Archibald, 75–7
Montherlant, Henri de, quoted, 10
Moore, Sybil, *see* Pope, Sybil
Moorehead, Alan, 48
Moran, Lord, 28
Mussolini, 83

Napier's history of the Peninsular War, 91–3

106, 107; exercises of 1934, 80; 1st Tank Brigade, 80, 81, 88–9, 100; 1st Battalion, 86–8; 4th Battalion, 86, 88; 6th Battalion, 86 *see also* Armoured cars

Royal Tank Regiment, 68, 74, 85, 140, 144; 3rd Battalion, 119, 121; 4th Battalion, 108; 4th/7th Battalion, 121, 6th Battalion, 53; 7th Battalion, 108

Royal Warwickshire Regiment, 7

Rundstedt, Field-Marshal von, 128

Russell, George (AE), 44–5

Russell, Brig Hugh, 139

Russian Relief Force (1919), 30–40; Russian Disciplinary Company and Battalion, 33–40

Russo-Polish War (1920), 52

Salisbury Plain manoeuvres (1931), 78

Sassoon, Siegfried, 8, 17

Scarpe, river, 114, 116, 117

Schweppenburg, Geyr von, 128

Second Army Corps (2 Corps) (1939–40), 101–7

Second Division (1940), 127

Self-propelled guns, 71

Seven Pillars of Wisdom (Lawrence), 38

Shaw, Bernard, 9

Sherman tank, 71, 129

Sidi Rezegh, 143, 145

Sinn Fein, 42, 46–50

Slim, Field-Marshal Visct, 2

Smith, Lieut-Gen Sir Arthur, 137, 138

Snelling, Major-Gen, 2

Somme river: battles of (First World War), 6, 19–20, 32; actions near (1940), 108, 110, 118–20

Sottingen, 108

Staff College, Camberley, 60–6

Stewart, Capt Baillie, 78n

Sweney, Brig, 21

Tank Board (1940), 125–7, 130

Tank Corps, 2, 5, 20, 43–5, 141; grant of prefix 'Royal', 58; 4th

Battalion, 43; 17th Battalion, 44, 19th Battalion, 43
see also Royal Tank Corps

'Tank Parliament' (1941), 134–135

Tanks, The (Liddell Hart), 59n, 70, 80, 86, 87n, 121n, 123, 138–139

10th Hussars, 141

3rd Division (1939), 102

13 Corps, *see* Eighth Army

13th/18th Hussars, 108

30 Corps, *see* Eighth Army

TIGER convoy, 136

Tilly, Brig Justice, 87, 106, 107

Tobruk, 1, 137, 142, 143

Tournai, 112, 113

Trenchard, Marshal of the Royal Air Force Viscount, 29, 53

12th Lancers, 86

Unwin, Brig Eric, 139

Valentine tank, 95, 145

Verney, Major-Gen, 85

Vickers Medium tank, 70n, 72

Vickers organization, 107n

Vimy Ridge, (1917), 21; (1940), 114–16, 120

Wahagnies, 108, 109, 116, 118

War in France and Flanders, The (Official Report), 119 and n

Wareham, 58, 59

Wavell, Field-Marshal Earl, 5, 97–101, 136–8

West Kent Regiment, 19

Westminster, Duke of, 52

Weygand, Gen, 115

White Russian forces, 30–1, 36, 37, 39

Willis, Rev Arthur, 4, 90

Winchester Repatriation Camp (1919), 29–30

Wingate, Major-Gen O. C., 75

Wireless telephones, use of, 72

Wyatt, Lieut-Col, 23

Ypres: Salient, 11–13, 15–16, 32; Third Battle of (1917), 22